VELVET ELVIS

Repainting the Christian Faith

ROB BELL

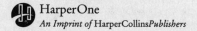

HarperOne
An Imprint of HarperCollins*Publishers*

HarperOne

HarperCollins books may be purchased for educational, business, or sales promotional use. For information please write: Special Markets Department, HarperCollins Publishers, 10 East 53rd Street, New York, NY 10022.

HarperCollins website: http://www.harpercollins.com

The story of Yvette on pages 87–88 is used with her permission.

Published in association with Yates & Yates, www.yates2.com.

FIRST PUBLISHED BY ZONDERVAN IN 2005

FIRST HARPERCOLLINS EDITION PUBLISHED IN 2012

Library of Congress Cataloging-in-Publication Data

Bell, Rob.
Velvet Elvis: repainting the Christian faith / Rob Bell.
p. cm.
Includes bibliographical references.
ISBN 978-0-06-219721-4
1. Christianity and culture. 2. Christian life. I. Title.
BR115.C8B395   2012
261—dc23
2012010236

12 13 14 15 16 RRD(H) 10 9 8 7 6 5 4 3 2 1

ACKNOWLEDGMENTS

I'm sending much love to all those who had a hand in this book:

Angela Scheff, editor extraordinaire

Chris Ferebee for staying calm

Erwin McManus for demanding that I write something before I die

Kent Dobson for reference help

Tom Maas for starting the car

My partners at Flannel for their tireless fidelity

René DeHaan-Canetti for teaching me more than he'll ever know

Tom Rinks for throwing the frisbee

The Mars Hill community—who would have thought?

My extended family for being up for the journey

Kristen, shall we go another eleven?

CONTENTS

WELCOME TO MY VELVET ELVIS

In my basement, behind some bikes and suitcases and boxes, sits a Velvet Elvis. A genuine, bought-by-the-side-of-the-road Velvet Elvis. And to say that this painting captures The King in all his glory would be an understatement. It's not the young Elvis—the thin one with the slicked-back hair in those black-and-white concert photos in which he's playing a guitar that's not plugged in. And it's not the old Elvis—the big one in the shiny cape singing to old women in Hawaii. My painting is the "Pre-doughnut Elvis."

A touch of blue in the hair; the tall, white collar that suggests one of those polyester jumpsuits; and those lips . . . if you stare long enough, you might even see them quiver.

But I think the best part of my Velvet Elvis is the lower left-hand corner, where the artist simply wrote a capital *R* and then a period.

R.

Because when you're this good, you don't even have to write your whole name.

What if, when the artist was done with this masterpiece, R. had announced there was no more need for anyone to paint, because he or she had just painted the ultimate painting? What if R. had held a press conference, unveiled his painting, and then called on all painters everywhere to put down their brushes, insisting that since the ultimate painting had been painted, there was simply no need for any of them to continue their work?

We would say that R. had lost his mind. We say this because we instinctively understand that art has to, in some way, keep going. Keep exploring, keep arranging, keep shaping and forming and bringing in new perspectives.

For thousands of years followers of Jesus, like artists, have understood that we have to keep going, exploring what it means to live in harmony with God and each other. The Christian faith tradition is filled with change and growth and transformation. Jesus took part in this process by calling people to rethink faith and the Bible and hope and love and everything else, and by inviting them into the endless process of working out how to live as God created us to live.

The challenge for Christians then is to live with great passion and conviction, remaining open and flexible, aware that this life is not the last painting.

Times change. God doesn't, but times do. We learn and grow, and the world around us shifts, and the Christian faith is alive only when it is listening, morphing, innovating, letting go of whatever has gotten in the way of Jesus and embracing whatever will help us be more and more the people God wants us to be.

There are endless examples of this ongoing process, so I'll describe just one. Around 500 years ago, a man named Martin Luther raised a whole series of questions about the painting the church was presenting to the world. He insisted that God's grace could not be purchased with money or good deeds. He wanted everyone to have their own copy of the Bible in a language they could read. He argued that everyone had a divine calling on their lives to serve God, not just priests who had jobs in churches. This concept was revolutionary for the world at that time. He was articulating earth-shattering ideas for his listeners. And they heard him. And something big, something historic, happened. Things changed. Thousands of people connected with God in ways they hadn't before.

But that wasn't the end of it. Luther was taking his place in a long line of people who never stopped rethinking and repainting the faith. Shedding unnecessary layers and at the same time rediscovering essentials that had been lost. Luther's work was part of what came to be called the Reformation. Because of this movement, the churches he was speaking against went through their own process of rethinking and repainting, making significant changes as a result.

And this process hasn't stopped.
It can't.

In fact, Luther's contemporaries used a very specific word for this endless, absolutely necessary process of change and growth. They didn't use the word *reformed*; they used the word *reforming*. This distinction is crucial. They knew that they and others hadn't gotten it perfect forever. They knew that the things they said and did and wrote and decided would need to be revisited. Rethought. Reworked.

I'm part of this tradition.

I'm part of this global, historic stream of people who believe that God has not left us alone but has been involved in human history from the beginning. People who believe that in Jesus, God came among us in a unique and powerful way, showing us a new kind of life. Giving each of us a new vision for our life together, for the world we live in.

And as a part of this tradition, I embrace the need to keep painting, to keep reforming.

By this I do not mean cosmetic, superficial changes like better lights and music, sharper graphics, and new methods with easy-to-follow steps. I mean theology: the beliefs about God, Jesus, the Bible, salvation, the future. We must keep reforming the way the Christian faith is defined, lived, and explained.

Jesus is more compelling than ever. More inviting, more true, more mysterious than ever. The problem isn't Jesus; the problem is what comes with Jesus.

For many people the word *Christian* conjures up all sorts of images that have nothing to do with who Jesus is and how he taught us to live. This must change.

For others, the painting works for their parents, or it provided meaning when they were growing up, but it is no longer relevant. It doesn't fit. It's outdated. It doesn't have anything to say to the world they live in every day. It's not that there isn't any truth in it or that all the people before them were misguided or missed the point. It's just that every generation has to ask the difficult questions of what it means to be a Christian here and now, in this place, at this time.

And if this difficult work isn't done, where does the painting end up?

In the basement.

Here's what often happens: Somebody comes along who has a fresh perspective on the Christian faith. People are inspired. A movement starts. Faith that was stale and dying is now alive. But then the pioneer of the movement—the painter—dies and the followers stop exploring. They mistakenly assume that their leader's words were the last ones on the subject, and they freeze their leader's words. They forget that as that innovator was doing his or her part to move things along, that person was merely taking part in the discussion that will go on forever. And so in their commitment to what so-and-so said and did, they end up freezing the faith.

What gets lost is the truth that whoever painted that version was just like us, searching for God and experiencing God and trying to get a handle on what the Christian faith looks like. And then a new generation comes along living in a new day and a new world, and they have to keep the tradition going or the previous paintings are going to end up in the basement.

The tradition then is painting, not making copies of the same painting over and over. The challenge of the art is to take what was great about the previous paintings and incorporate that into new paintings.

And in the process, make something beautiful—for today.

For many Christians, the current paintings are enough. The churches, the books, the language, the methods, the beliefs—there is nothing wrong with it. It works for them and meets their needs, and they gladly invite others to join them in it. I thank God for that. I celebrate those who have had their lives transformed in these settings.

But this book is for those who need a fresh take on Jesus and what it means to live the kind of life he teaches us to live. I'm part of a community, a movement of people who have been living, exploring, discussing, sharing, and experiencing new understandings of Christian faith.

And we love it. We are alive in ways we never thought possible. We are caught up in something we gladly give our lives to. This is the place that I write from: a place of joy and freedom, as a member of a community wanting to invite others to come along on the journey. We are just getting started. I have as many questions as answers, and I'm convinced that we're only scratching the surface. What I do know is that this pursuit of Jesus is leading us backward as much as forward.

If it is true, then it isn't new.

I am learning that what seems brand new is often the discovery of something that's been there all along—it just got lost somewhere and it needs to be picked up, dusted off, and reclaimed. I am learning that I come from a tradition that has wrestled with the deepest questions of human existence for thousands of years. I am learning that my tradition includes the rabbis and reformers and revolutionaries and monks and nuns and pastors and writers and philosophers and artists and every person everywhere who has asked big questions of a big God.

Welcome to my Velvet Elvis.

MOVEMENT ONE

JUMP

Several years ago my parents and in-laws gave our boys a trampoline. A fifteen-footer with netting around the outside so kids don't end up headfirst in the flowers. Since then my boys and I have logged more hours on that trampoline than I could begin to count. When we first got it, my older son, who was five at the time, discovered that if he timed his bounce with mine, he could launch higher than if he was jumping on his own.

I remember the first time he called my wife, Kristen, out into the backyard to watch him jump off of my bounce. Now mind you, up until this point he was maybe getting a foot higher because of his new technique. But this one particular time, when my wife was watching for the first time, something freakish happened in the space-time continuum. When he jumped, there was this perfect convergence of his weight and my weight and his jump and my jump, and I'm sure barometric pressure and air temperature had something to do with it too, because he went really high.

I don't mean a few feet off the mat. I mean he went over my head. Forty pounds of boy, clawing the air like a cat thrown from a second-story window, and a man making eye contact with his wife and thinking, *This is not good.*

She told us she didn't think our new trick was very safe and we should be careful. Which we were.

Until she went inside the house.

It is on this trampoline that God has started to make more sense to me. Because when it comes to faith, everybody has it. People often tell me they could never have faith, that it is just too hard. The idea that some people have faith and others don't is a popular one. But it is not a true one. Everybody has faith. Everybody is following somebody. What often happens is that people with specific beliefs about God end up backed into a corner, defending their faith against the calm, cool rationality of others. As if they have faith and beliefs and others don't.

But that is not true. Let's take an example: Some people believe we were made by a creator who has plans and purposes for his creation, while others believe there is no greater meaning to life, no grand design, and we exist not because of some divine intention but because of random chance. This is not a discussion between people of faith and people who don't have faith. Both perspectives are faith perspectives, built on systems of belief. The person who says we are here by chance and there is no greater meaning has just as many beliefs as the person who says there's a creator. Maybe even more.

Think about some of the words that are used in these kinds of discussions, one of the most common being the phrase "open-minded." Often the person with spiritual convictions is seen as close-minded and others are seen as open-minded. What is fascinating to me is that at the center of the Christian faith is the assumption that this life isn't all there is. That there is more to life than the material. That existence is not limited to what we can see, touch, measure, taste, hear, and observe. One of the central assertions of the Christian worldview is that there is "more."[1] Those who oppose this insist that this is all there is, that only what we can measure and observe and see with our eyes is real. There is nothing else. Which perspective is more "closed-minded"? Which perspective is more "open"?

An atheist is a person of tremendous faith. In our discussions about the things that matter most then, we aren't talking about faith or no faith. Belief or no belief. We are talking about faith in what? Belief in what? The real question isn't whether we have it or not, but what we have put it in.

Everybody follows somebody. All of us make decisions every day about what is important, how to treat people, and what to do with our lives. These decisions come from what we believe about every aspect of our existence. And we got our beliefs from somewhere. We have been formed, every one of us, by this complicated mix of people and places and things. Parents and teachers and artists and scientists and mentors—we are each taking all of these influences and living our lives according to which teachings we have made our own. Some insist that they aren't influenced by any person or any religion, that they think for themselves. And that's an honorable perspective. The problem is they got that perspective from . . . somebody. They're following somebody even if they insist it is themselves they are following.

Everybody is following somebody. Everybody has faith in something and somebody.

We are all believers.

Way

As a Christian, I am simply trying to orient myself around living a particular kind of way, the kind of way that Jesus taught is possible. And I think that the way of Jesus is the best possible way to live.

This isn't irrational or primitive or blind faith. It is merely being honest that we all are living a "way."

I'm convinced being generous is a better way to live.
I'm convinced forgiving people and not carrying around bitterness is a better way to live.
I'm convinced having compassion is a better way to live.

I'm convinced pursuing peace in every situation is a
better way to live.
I'm convinced listening to the wisdom of others is a
better way to live.
I'm convinced being honest with people is a better way
to live.

This way of thinking isn't weird or strange; it is simply
acknowledging that everybody follows somebody, and
I'm trying to follow Jesus.

Over time when you purposefully try to live the way of
Jesus, you start noticing something deeper going on. You
begin realizing the reason this is the best way to live is
that it is rooted in profound truths about how the world
is. You find yourself living more and more in tune with
ultimate reality. You are more and more in sync with how
the universe is at its deepest levels.

Jesus's intention was, and is, to call people to live in tune
with reality. He said at one point that if you had seen him,
you had "seen the Father."[2] He claimed to be showing us
what God is like. In his compassion, peace, truth telling,
and generosity, he was showing us God.

And God is the ultimate reality. There is nothing more
beyond God.

Jesus at one point claimed to be "the way, the truth, and
the life." Jesus was not making claims about one religion
being better than all other religions. That completely

misses the point, the depth, and the truth. Rather, he was telling those who were following him that his way is the way to the depth of reality. This kind of life Jesus was living, perfectly and completely in connection and cooperation with God, is the best possible way for a person to live. It is how things are.

Jesus exposes us to reality at its rawest.

So the way of Jesus is not about religion; it's about reality.

It's about lining yourself up with how things are.[3]

Perhaps a better question than who's right, is who's living rightly?

Springs

This is where the springs on the trampoline come in. When we jump, we begin to see the need for springs. The springs help make sense of these deeper realities that drive how we live every day. The springs aren't God. The springs aren't Jesus. The springs are statements and beliefs *about* our faith that help give words to the depth that we are experiencing in our jumping. I would call these the doctrines of the Christian faith.

They aren't the point.

They help us understand the point, but they are a means and not an end. We take them seriously, and at the same time we keep them in proper perspective.

Take, for example, the doctrine—the spring—called the Trinity. This doctrine is central to historic, orthodox Christian faith. While there is only one God, God is somehow present everywhere. People began to call this presence, this power of God, his "Spirit." So there is God, and then there is God's Spirit. And then Jesus comes among us and has this oneness with God that has people saying things like God has visited us in the flesh.[4] So God is one, but God has also revealed himself to us as Spirit and then as Jesus. One and yet three. This three-in-oneness understanding of God emerged in the several hundred years after Jesus's resurrection. People began to call this concept the Trinity. The word *trinity* is not found anywhere in the Bible. Jesus didn't use the word, and the writers of the rest of the Bible didn't use the word. But over time this belief, this understanding, this doctrine, has become central to how followers of Jesus have understood who God is. It is a spring, and people jumped for thousands of years without it.[5] It was added later. We can take it out and examine it. Discuss it, probe it, question it. It flexes, and it stretches.

In fact, its stretch and flex are what make it so effective. It is firmly attached to the frame and the mat, yet it has room to move. And it has brought a fuller, deeper, richer understanding to the mysterious being who is God.

Once again, the springs aren't God. They have emerged over time as people have discussed and studied and experienced and reflected on their growing understanding of who God is. Our words aren't absolutes. Only God is absolute, and God has no intention of sharing this absoluteness with anything, especially words people have come up with to talk about him. This is something people have struggled with since the beginning: how to talk about God when God is bigger than our words, our brains, our worldviews, and our imaginations.

In the book of Deuteronomy, Moses reminds the people that when they encountered God, they "heard the sound of words but saw no form."[6]

No form, no shape.
Nothing you could see.

In Moses's day, the way you honored and respected whatever gods you followed was by making carvings or sculptures of them and then bowing down to what you had made. These were gods you could get your mind around. Moses is confronting people with an entirely new concept of what the true God is like. He is claiming that no statue or carving could ever capture this God, because this God has no shape or form.

This was a revolutionary idea in the history of religion.

You are holding a book in your hands. It has shape and volume and weight and all the stuff that makes it a thing.

It has thingness.

This book has edges and boundaries that define it as a finite thing. It is a book and nothing else.

But the writers of the Bible go to great lengths to describe God as a being with no edges or boundaries or limits. God has no thingness because there's no end to God.

Or as the question goes in the book of Job: "Can you probe the limits of the Almighty?"[7]

It makes sense, then, in a strange sort of way, that when Moses asks God for his name, God replies, "I am."[8]

Doesn't really clear things up, does it?

Moses is looking for a being he can wrap his mind around. Is this the god of water or power or soil or fertility? All the other gods *made sense;* you could *understand* them— who they were and what they did and what they stood for. But this God is different. Mysterious. Unfathomable.

"I am."

The name's origins come from the verb *to be,* so some read it as "I will be who I will be."

Others suggest it should be read like this: "I always have been, I am, and I always will be."

Perhaps this is God's way of saying, "If your goal is to figure me out and totally understand me, it's not going to happen. Even my name is more than you can comprehend."

Later Moses says to God, "Now show me your glory."

Which is our way of saying, "I need more. I need something I can see. Something tangible."

God's response? He tells Moses to go stand on a rock, because he's going to pass by. He explains to Moses that no one can see him and live, so he'll cover Moses with his hand (God's hand?) as he passes by, and then he says, "I will remove my hand and you will see my back."[9]

The ancient rabbis had all sorts of things to say about this passage, but one of the most fascinating things they picked up on is the part about God's back. They argued that in the original Hebrew language, the word *back* should be understood as a euphemism for "where I just was."

It is as if God is saying, "The best you're going to do, the most you are capable of, is seeing where I . . . just . . . was."

That's the closest you are going to get.

If there is a divine being who made everything, including us, what would our experiences with this being look like? The moment God is figured out with nice neat lines and definitions, we are no longer dealing with God. We are dealing with somebody we made up. And if we made him up, then we are in control. And so in passage after passage, we find God reminding people that he is beyond and bigger and more.

This truth about God is why study and discussion and doctrines are so necessary. They help us put words to realities beyond words. They give us insight and understanding into the experience of God we're having. Which is why the springs only work when they serve the greater cause: us finding our lives in God. If they ever become the point, something has gone seriously wrong. Doctrine is a wonderful servant and a horrible master.

The springs are huge—they hold up the mat—but they aren't God. They aren't Jesus.

Bricks

Somebody recently gave me a videotape of a lecture given by a man who travels around speaking about the creation of the world. At one point in his lecture, he said if you deny that God created the world in six literal twenty-four-hour days, then you are denying that Jesus ever died on the cross.[10] It's a bizarre leap of logic to make, I would say.

But he was serious.

It hit me while I was watching that for him faith isn't a trampoline; it's a wall of bricks. Each of the core doctrines for him is like an individual brick that stacks on top of the others. If you pull one out, the whole wall starts to crumble. It appears quite strong and rigid, but if you begin to rethink or discuss even one brick, the whole thing is in danger. Like he said, no six-day creation equals no cross. Remove one, and the whole wall wobbles.

What if tomorrow someone digs up definitive proof that Jesus had a real, earthly, biological father named Larry, and archaeologists find Larry's tomb and do DNA samples and prove beyond a shadow of a doubt that the virgin birth was really just a bit of mythologizing the Gospel writers threw in to appeal to the followers of the Mithra and Dionysian religious cults that were hugely popular at the time of Jesus, whose gods had virgin births? But what if as you study the origin of the word *virgin*, you discover that the word *virgin* in the gospel of Matthew actually comes from the book of Isaiah, and then you find out that in the Hebrew language at that time, the word *virgin* could mean several things. And what if you discover that in the first century being "born of a virgin" also referred to a child whose mother became pregnant the first time she had intercourse?

What if that spring was seriously questioned?

Could a person keep jumping? Could a person still love God? Could you still be a Christian?

Is the way of Jesus still the best possible way to live?

Or does the whole thing fall apart?

I affirm the historic Christian faith, which includes the virgin birth and the Trinity and the inspiration of the Bible and much more. I'm a part of it, and I want to pass it on to the next generation. I believe that God created everything and that Jesus is Lord and that God has plans to restore everything.[11]

But if the whole faith falls apart when we reexamine and rethink one spring, then it wasn't that strong in the first place, was it?

This is because a brick is fixed in size. It can't flex or change size, because if it does, then it can't fit into the wall. What happens then is that the wall becomes the sum total of the beliefs, and God becomes as big as the wall. But God is bigger than any wall. God is bigger than any religion. God is bigger than any worldview. God is bigger than the Christian faith.

This truth clicked for me last Friday in a new way. Somebody showed me a letter from the president of a large seminary who is raising money to help him train leaders who will defend Christianity. The letter went on about the desperate need for defense of the true faith. What disturbed me was the defensive posture of the letter, which reflects one of the things that happens in brickworld: you spend a lot of time talking about how right you are. Which of course leads to how wrong everybody else is. Which then leads to defending the wall. It struck me reading the letter that you rarely defend a trampoline. You invite people to jump on it with you.

I am far more interested in jumping than I am in arguing about whose trampoline is better. You rarely defend the things you love. You enjoy them and tell others about them and invite others to enjoy them with you.

Have you ever seen someone pull a photo out of their wallet and argue about the supremacy of this particular loved one? Of course not. They show you the picture and give you the opportunity to see what they see.

The first Christians announced this way of Jesus as "the good news." That tells me the invitation is for everybody. The problem with brickianity is that walls inevitably keep people out. Often it appears as though you have to agree with all of the bricks exactly as they are or you can't join. Maybe you have been outside the wall before. You know exactly what I'm talking about.

Jesus talks about this "in and out" a lot in his teachings. He keeps insisting that the people who assume they are in may not be in and the ones who everybody thinks are out for whatever reason may in fact be in. In one parable, he has the Judge of Everything telling some religious people, "Depart from me, for I never knew you."[12] Stunning. And in another parable, a man has a feast and none of his invited guests come, so he sends word to all the marginalized, disgusting, unclean people who are "out" that they are invited to come "in" and celebrate with him.[13] Again, stunning.

Jesus invites everybody to jump.

And saying yes to the invitation doesn't mean we have to have it all figured out. This is an important thing to remember: I can jump and still have questions and doubts. I often meet people who are waiting to follow God until they have all their questions answered. They will be waiting for a long time, because if we knew everything, we'd be . . . God. So the invitation to jump is an invitation to follow Jesus with all of our doubts and questions right there with us.

Questions

A Christian doesn't avoid the questions; a Christian embraces them. In fact, to truly pursue the living God, we have to see the *need* for questions.

Questions are not scary.
What is scary is when people don't have any.
What is tragic is faith that has no room for them.

We sponsored a Doubt Night at our church awhile back. People were encouraged to write down whatever questions or doubts they had about God and Jesus and the Bible and faith and church. We had to get a large box to hold all of the scraps of paper. The first question was from a woman who had been raped and didn't press charges because she was told that doing so wasn't "the Christian thing to do." The man then raped several other girls, and this woman wanted to know if God would still forgive her even if she hadn't forgiven the man who raped her.

Did I mention that this was the first question? Here are a few more asked that night:

"Why does God let people die . . . so young?"
"Why does it seem that mean people get the most money?"
"Why does the killer go free and the honest man die of cancer?"
"Sometimes I doubt God's presence in starving Africa."
"If we can ask God for forgiveness at our last breath, why strive for a godly life in the present?"
"Either God is in control of everything and so all the crap we see today is part of his plan (which I don't want to accept), or it's all out of control (which sucks too). What's up?"

This is just a random sampling. I have page after page of questions on my desk. Heaven and hell and suicide and the devil and God and love and rape—some very personal, some angry, some desperate, some very deep and philosophical.

Most of my responses were about how we need others to carry our burdens and how our real needs in life are not for more information but for loving community with other people on the journey. But what was so powerful for those I spoke with was that they were free to voice what was deepest in their hearts and minds. Questions, doubts, struggles. It wasn't the information that helped them—it was simply being in an environment in which they were free to voice what was inside.

And this is why questions are so central to faith. A question by its very nature acknowledges that the person asking the question does not have all of the answers. And because the person does not have all of the answers, they are looking outside of themselves for guidance.

Questions, no matter how shocking or blasphemous or arrogant or ignorant or raw, are rooted in humility. A humility that understands that I am not God. And there is more to know.

Questions bring freedom. Freedom that I don't have to be God and I don't have to pretend that I have it all figured out. I can let God be God.[14]

In the book of Genesis, God tells Abraham what he is going to do with Sodom and Gomorrah, and Abraham fires back, "Will not the Ruler of the earth do right?"

Abraham thinks God is in the wrong and the proposed action is not in line with who God is, and Abraham questions him about it. Actually, they get into a sort of bargaining discussion in which Abraham doesn't let up. He keeps questioning God. And God not only doesn't get angry, but he seems to engage with Abraham all the more.[15]

Maybe that is who God is looking for—people who don't just sit there and mindlessly accept whatever comes their way.

Moses tries for two chapters to convince God that he has picked the wrong man, and God seems all the more convinced with each question that he has picked the right man.[16]

David says this to God in Psalm 13: "How long, Lord? Will you forget me forever? How long will you hide your face from me? How long must I wrestle with my thoughts and day after day have sorrow in my heart? How long will my enemy triumph over me? Look on me and answer."

What's the first thing Mary says to the angel who brings her the news that she's going to be the mother of the Messiah?

"But how can this be? I'm a virgin!"
Questions. Questions. Questions.

What are some of Jesus's final words? "My God, my God, why have you forsaken me?"

Jesus. On the cross. Questioning God.

Central to the Christian experience is the art of questioning God. Not belligerent, arrogant questions that have no respect for our maker, but naked, honest, vulnerable, raw questions, arising out of the awe that comes from engaging the living God.

This type of questioning frees us. Frees us from having to have it all figured out. Frees us from having answers to everything. Frees us from always having to be right. It allows us to have moments when we come to the end of our ability to comprehend. Moments when the silence is enough.

The great Abraham Joshua Heschel once said, "I did not ask for success, I asked for wonder."[17]

The Christian faith is mysterious to the core. It is about things and beings that ultimately can't be put into words. Language fails. And if we do definitively put God into words, we have at that very moment made God something God is not.

Most of us are conditioned to think of mystery in terms of a television show or a novel or a film in which the mystery is solved at the end.[18] Often right before the credits we find out who did it, or who is actually the long-lost son of whom, or that she is actually a he. Or that Bruce Willis was dead for most of the movie and we just now figured it out.[19]

Mystery is created when key facts are hidden from the viewer. What the writer/director/creator does at the end is pull back the curtain and show us the things that had previously been hidden.

So the mystery gets solved and our questions get answered.

But the Bible has an entirely different understanding of mystery. True mystery, the kind of mystery rooted in the infinite nature of God, gives us answers that actually plunge us into even more . . . questions.

Take this example from John 3:16. The first part of the verse reads: "For God so loved the world that he gave his one and only Son."

So why did God give his son?
Because God loves the world.
But what does it mean for God to love the world?

Does God love evil people? Mean people? People who don't think that God exists? People who think that God loves only them? If you do enough evil, can you exhaust God's love?

Because God loves the world *is* an answer to the question, why did God give his son? It's a real answer; it's an answer you can trust; it's an answer you can base your life on. It's an answer you can know. But it also raises a new set of questions.

Why does God love the world?
What motivates God to love like this? What does God get out of it?

The writers of the Bible, especially one named John, would answer this way: "Because God *is* love."[20]

Which is an answer, of course, but as you probably have figured out by now, it raises even deeper questions: How can God *be* love? Is every experience of love an experience of God? Is every experience of God an experience of love?

So God is love is an answer to the question, why does God love the world? But as an answer, it raises even more questions. And we could go on and on and on.

Truth always leads to more . . . truth. Because truth is insight into God and God is infinite and God has no boundaries or edges. So truth always has layers and depth and texture.

It's like a pool that you dive into, and you start swimming toward the bottom, and soon you discover that no matter how hard and fast you swim downward, the pool keeps getting . . . deeper. The bottom will always be out of reach.

One of the great "theologians" of our time, Sean Penn, put it this way: "When everything gets answered, it's fake. The mystery *is* the truth."[21]

The mystery *is* the truth.

Or take the Trinity, for example. Even the best definitions end up sounding like a small child trying to play Mozart on pots and pans in the middle of the kitchen floor. The more you study the Trinity and what has been said about it over the years, the more you are left in wonder and awe about the nature of God.

As one of my friends often says: "If you study the Bible and it doesn't lead you to wonder and awe, then you haven't studied the Bible."[22]

The very nature of orthodox Christian faith is that we never come to the end. It begs for more. More discussion, more inquiry, more debate, more questions.

It's not so much that the Christian faith *has* a lot of paradoxes. It's that it *is* a lot paradoxes. And we cannot resolve a paradox. We have to let it be what it is.

Being a Christian then is more about celebrating mystery than conquering it.

The Eastern church father Gregory of Nyssa talked about Moses's journey up Mount Sinai in Exodus 19. When Moses enters the darkness toward the top of the mountain, he has moved beyond knowledge to awe and to love and to the mystery of God. Gregory insists that Moses has not arrived when he enters the darkness of the mountaintop. His journey and exploration have only really begun.[23]

Which leads to a really obvious observation: A trampoline only works if you take your feet off the firm, stable ground and jump into the air and let the trampoline propel you upward. Talking about trampolines isn't jumping; it's talking. Two vastly different things. And so we jump and we invite others to jump with us, to live the way of Jesus and see what happens. You don't have to know anything about the springs to pursue living "the way."

In brickworld, the focus often becomes getting people to believe the right things so they can be "in." There is often a list of however many doctrines, and the goal is to get people to intellectually assent to these things being true. Once we believe the right things, then we're in. And once we're in, the goal often becomes learning how to get others in with us. I know this is harsh, but in many settings it is true. It is possible in these settings to be in, and to believe all of the correct things, and even to be effective at getting others in, and yet our hearts can remain unaffected. It's possible to believe all the right things and be miserable. It's possible to believe all the right doctrines and not live as Jesus teaches us to live. This is why I am so passionate about the trampoline. I want to invite people to actually live this way so the life Jesus offers gradually becomes their life. It becomes less and less about talking, and more and more about the experience we are actually having.

And what is the point, while we're at it, of a trampoline?

Joy

The point is our joy. That is when God is most pleased.[24] They aren't two different things: God's joy over here and our joy over there. They are the same. God takes great pleasure in us living as we were made to live. He even commands it in the Psalms: "Take delight in the Lord."[25] It's such an odd command, isn't it? You will be happy or else. But God is serious about this. Now this joy doesn't rule out suffering, difficulty, and struggle. In fact, taking Jesus seriously almost guarantees that our lives will be difficult. History proves it. And very few actually set out to live such a focused, beautiful life. Narrow is the way, and only a few find it.[26] But the kind of joy God speaks of transcends these struggles and difficulties. I love how one writer put it: "The peace of God, which transcends all understanding."[27]

Sometimes when my boys and I are jumping and one of us starts laughing, we all start laughing. We're jumping and we're short of breath and we're sweating and we're having such a great time. When we're too exhausted to jump anymore, we'll lie down on the mat and stare up at the vast blue sky above us and watch the clouds go by and listen to the breeze as it moves the leaves overhead. I'll be there on my back, and I'll say a short prayer: "God, I can't believe I get to live this life."

YOKE

Please understand, I stumbled into this gig.

I was teaching waterskiing the summer after I graduated from college at a camp in northern Wisconsin called Honey Rock. My job was to drive the boat all day, drag kids around the lake, plan ski shows, and get paid $30 a week for it. Every Sunday morning the camp had a chapel service in the middle of pine trees beside the lake. One week I was with the people who were planning the service, and for some reason, when they started discussing who would give the message, I told them I would do it. I had never preached or taught or tried to explain the Bible to a group of people—I had absolutely no idea what I was doing.

And they said, "You're on this Sunday."

I walked around the woods a lot that week, asking God to give me something to say. And if God could give it to me before Sunday, that would be great.

Sunday eventually came. I remember standing up to talk in front of those hundred or so people gathered among those pine trees and being aware of the presence of God in a terrifying way. Seriously, it was terrifying. But in a good way. The word that comes to mind is *holy.* I became aware of something so real, yet I couldn't see it or touch it. I was standing there and I hadn't said a word yet, and what did I do? I took off my sandals because I knew the ground I was standing on was holy and that my life was never, ever going to be the same again.

It was in that moment that I heard a voice. Not an audible, loud, human kind of voice, but inner words spoken somewhere in my soul that were very clear and very concise. What I heard was, "Teach this book, and I will take care of everything else."

In that moment, my entire life changed forever. It was like a rebirth. I had been so restless and rebellious and unsettled and unfocused, and I had all this energy and passion but nowhere to channel it. Now I had something I could do with my life. In that moment by the side of a lake, barefoot, with my tongue tied and my heart on fire, I found something I could give my life to.

Or it found me.

It wasn't planned. No angels were involved that I know of—just a young, restless soul discovering a purpose.

Like I said, I stumbled into this gig.

So for a little over ten years, I have oriented my life around studying, reading, teaching, and trying to understand the Bible. I continue to find the Bible the most mysterious book—the more insight I gain, the more I realize how much I don't know. It inspires and encourages, and it also frustrates and provokes.

The Bible is a difficult book.

It's Difficult

We all understand that ethnic cleansing is evil, and when someone announces that God has told him or her to kill certain people, we think that person is crazy. And yet there are passages in the Bible in which God orders "his" people to kill innocent women and children. The famous story of the people marching around the wall of Jericho, blowing their horns, and then the walls falling down is also a story about slaughter of the innocent. The text reads, "They devoted the city to the Lord and destroyed with the sword every living thing in it—men and women, young and old, cattle, sheep and donkeys." The section ends with this verse: "So the Lord was with Joshua."[1]

God was with Joshua when he killed all those women and children?
Is God really like that?
What does a thinking, honest person do with a story like this?

And while we're at it, what about those letters in the New Testament from one person to another group of people? Notice this verse from 2 Corinthians: "I am out of my mind to talk like this."[2] A man named Paul is writing this, so is it his word or God's word?

Is God out of his mind?
Is God out of Paul's mind?
Is Paul out of God's mind?
Or does it simply mean that Paul is out of Paul's mind?

And if the verse is simply Paul being out of Paul's mind, then how is *that* God's word?

Notice this verse from 1 Corinthians: "To the rest I say this (I, not the Lord) . . ."[3] Here we have Paul writing to a group of Christians, and he wants to make it clear that the next thing he is going to say comes from him, "not the Lord."

So when a writer of the Bible makes it clear that what he is writing comes straight from him, how is that still the word of God?

Now I think the Bible is the most amazing, beautiful, deep, inspired, engaging collection of writings ever. How is it that this ancient book continues to affect me in ways no other book does?

But sometimes when I hear people quote the Bible, I just want to throw up.

Can I just say that?
Can I get that off my chest?

Sometimes when people are backing up their points and the Bible is used to prove that they are right, everything within me says, "There is no way that's what God meant by that verse."

Several hundred years ago people used Bible verses to defend their right to own slaves.

Recently a woman told me that she has the absolute Word of God (the Bible) and that the "opinions of man" don't mean a thing to her. But this same woman would also tell you that she has a personal relationship with God through Jesus. In fact, she spends a great deal of time telling people they need a personal relationship with God through Jesus. What is interesting to me is that the phrase "personal relationship" isn't found anywhere in the Bible. Someone made up this phrase and then said you could have one with God. Apparently the "opinions of man" do mean something to her.

I was reading last year in one of the national news magazines about a gathering of the leaders of a massive Christian denomination (literally millions of members worldwide). The reason their annual gathering was in the news was that they had voted to reaffirm their view of the importance of the verse that says a wife's role is to submit to her husband.

This is a big deal to them.
This is what made news.
This is what they are known for.
What about the verse before that verse?
What about the verse after it?
What about the verse that talks about women having authority over their husbands?[4]
What about all of the marriages in which this verse has been used to oppress and mistreat women?
It is possible to make the Bible say whatever we want it to, isn't it?

How is it that the Bible can be so many different things to so many different people?

Nazis, cult leaders, televangelists who promise that God will bless you if you just get out your checkbook, racists, people who oppress minorities and the poor and anyone not like them—they all can find verses in the Bible to back up their agendas.

We have all heard the Bible used in certain ways and found ourselves asking, "Oh God, you couldn't have meant that, could you?"

Somebody recently told me, "As long as you teach the Bible, I have no problem with you."

Think about that for a moment.

What that person was really saying is, "As long as you teach *my version* of the Bible, I'll have no problem with you." And the more people insist that they are just taking the Bible for what it says, the more skeptical I get.

Which for me raises one huge question: Is the Bible the best God can do?

With God being so massive and awe-inspiring and full of truth, why is his book capable of so much confusion?

Why did God do it this way?

Where does one go in trying to make sense of what the Bible even is, let alone what it says?

For me, clarity has begun to emerge when I've begun to understand what Jesus believed about the scriptures.

Let's start with a straightforward verse from the book of Leviticus: "Do not seek revenge or bear a grudge against anyone among your people, but love your neighbor as yourself. I am the Lord."[5]

Could there be a more basic verse? "Love your neighbor as yourself."

Who could possibly have any sort of problem with this verse?
And how could someone mess this up?
What could be complicated about loving your neighbor?

Even people who don't believe in God and don't read the Bible would say that loving your neighbor is a good thing to do.

A couple of questions this verse raises: How do we live this verse out? What does it mean to love? What isn't love? Who decides what is love and what isn't love?

And what about your neighbor? Who is your neighbor? Is your neighbor only the person next door, or is it anyone you have contact with? Or is it every single human being on the face of the planet?

And what happens if one person's definition of love and another person's definition differ? Who is right? Who is wrong? Who decides who is right and who is wrong? Who decides if whoever decided made the right decision?

So even a verse as basic as this raises more questions than it answers.

In order to live it out and not just talk about it, someone somewhere has to make decisions about this verse. Someone has to decide what it actually looks like to put flesh and blood on this command.

And that's because the Bible is open-ended.

It *has* to be interpreted. And if it isn't interpreted, then it can't be put into action. So if we are serious about following God, then we have to interpret the Bible. It is not possible to simply do what the Bible says. We must first make decisions about what it means at this time, in this place, for these people.

Here's another example from the Torah (the Jewish name for the first five books of the Bible): "Remember the Sabbath day by keeping it holy."[6] The next verses command the people to do no work on this Sabbath day; they then explain the command by saying that God rested on the seventh day after creating the world in the first six days.

You can already see the questions this verse raises: Who defines work? Who defines rest? What if work to one person is rest to another? What if rest to one person is work to another? And what *does* it mean to make a day *holy*? How do you know if you've kept something holy? How would you know if you hadn't?

Once again, the Bible is open-ended. It has to be interpreted.

Somebody has to decide what it means to love your neighbor, and somebody has to decide what it means to observe the Sabbath and keep it holy.

Rabbis

Now the ancient rabbis understood that the Bible is open-ended and has to be interpreted. And they understood that their role in the community was to study and meditate and discuss and pray and then make those decisions. Rabbis are like interpreters, helping people understand what God is saying to them through the text and what it means to live out the text.

Take for example the Sabbath command in Exodus. A rabbi would essentially put actions in two categories: things the rabbi permitted on the Sabbath and things the rabbi forbade on the Sabbath. The rabbi was driven by a desire to get as close as possible to what God originally intended in the command at hand. One rabbi might say that you could walk so far on the Sabbath, but if you went farther, that would be work and you would be violating the Sabbath. Another might permit you to walk farther but forbid you to do certain actions another rabbi might permit.

Different rabbis had different sets of rules, which were really different lists of what they forbade and what they permitted. A rabbi's set of rules and lists, which was really that rabbi's interpretation of how to live the Torah, was called that rabbi's yoke. When you followed a certain rabbi, you were following him because you believed that rabbi's set of interpretations were the closest to what God intended through the scriptures. And when you followed that rabbi, you were taking up that rabbi's yoke.

One rabbi even said his yoke was easy.[7]

The intent then of a rabbi having a yoke wasn't just to interpret the words correctly; it was to live them out. In the Jewish context, action was always the goal. It still is.

Rabbis would spend hours discussing with their students what it meant to live out a certain text. If a student made a suggestion about what a certain text meant and the rabbi thought the student had totally missed the point, the rabbi would say, "You have abolished the Torah," which meant that in the rabbi's opinion, the student wasn't anywhere near what God wanted. But if the student got it right, if the rabbi thought the student had grasped God's intention in the text, the rabbi would say, "You have fulfilled the Torah."

Notice what Jesus says in one of his first messages: "I have not come to abolish [the Torah] but to fulfill [it]."[8] He was essentially saying, "I didn't come to do away with the words of God; I came to show people what it looks like when the Torah is lived out perfectly, right down to the smallest punctuation marks."

"I'm here to put flesh and blood on the words."[9]

Most rabbis taught the yoke of a well respected rabbi who had come before them. So if you visited a synagogue and the local rabbi (Torah teacher) was going to teach, you might hear that this rabbi teaches in the name of Rabbi So-and-So. If you were familiar with the yoke of Rabbi So-and-So, then you would know what to expect from this rabbi.

Every once in a while, a rabbi would come along who was teaching a new yoke, a new way of interpreting the Torah. This was rare and extraordinary.

Imagine: A rabbi was claiming that he had a new way to understand the scriptures that was closer to what God intended than the way of the rabbis who had come before him. A new take on the scriptures.

The questions would immediately be raised: "How do we know this is truth? How do we know this rabbi isn't crazy?" One of the protections for the rabbi in this case was that two other rabbis with authority would lay hands on the rabbi and essentially validate him. They would be saying, "We believe this rabbi has authority to make new interpretations." That's why Jesus's baptism was so important. John the Baptist was a powerful teacher and prophet who was saying publicly that he wasn't worthy to carry Jesus's sandals.[10]

"And a voice from heaven said, 'This is my Son, whom I love; with him I am well pleased.'"[11]

A second voice affirmed Jesus's unique calling. The voice of God.

Amazing.

A Jewish audience reading Matthew's account of Jesus's baptism would pick up right away on Jesus's getting the affirmation of two powerful voices.[12]

Which leads to an interesting scene: In the book of Luke, what is the one question the religious leaders keep hounding Jesus with?

"Where did you get your authority?"

Jesus's response? "You tell me, where did John get his?"[13]

Now imagine if a rabbi who had a new perspective on the Torah was coming to town. This rabbi who was making new interpretations of the Torah was said to have authority. The Hebrew word for "authority" is *shmikah.* This might not even happen in your lifetime. You would hike for miles to hear him.

A rabbi who taught with *shmikah* would say things like, "You have heard it said . . . , but I tell you. . . ."[14]

What he was saying is, "You have heard people interpret that verse this way, but I tell you that this is what God really means in that verse."

Now the rabbis had technical terms for this endless process of forbidding and permitting and making interpretations. They called it "binding and loosing." To "bind" something was to forbid it. To "loose" something was to allow it.[15]

So a rabbi would bind certain practices and loose other practices. And when he gave his disciples the authority to bind and loose, it was called "giving the keys of the kingdom."

Notice what Jesus says in the book of Matthew: "I will give you the keys of the kingdom of heaven; whatever you bind on earth will be bound in heaven, and whatever you loose on earth will be loosed in heaven."[16]

What he is doing here is significant. He is giving his followers the authority to make *new* interpretations of the Bible. He is giving them permission to say, "Hey, we think we missed it before on that verse, and we've recently come to the conclusion that this is what it actually means."

And not only is he giving them authority, but he is saying that when they do debate and discuss and pray and wrestle and then make decisions about the Bible, somehow God in heaven will be involved.

Our Turn

Jesus expects his followers to be engaged in the endless process of deciding what it means to actually live the scriptures. And right away in the life of this new movement, we see them doing it. In Acts 15, these first Christians find themselves having to make a huge decision about what it means to be a Christian.

To understand what they are facing, we have to understand that they are Jewish—Jewish believers who are circumcised and eat kosher and recite Jewish prayers and celebrate Jewish feasts.

Jewish followers of a Jewish messiah who live a Jewish life in a Jewish nation.

But all sorts of Gentiles (people who aren't Jewish) start becoming followers of Jesus. People who don't eat kosher, who aren't circumcised, who don't dress and talk and look and live like them.

So what do they do? Do they expect all of these Gentiles to start being Jewish?

And what exactly would that mean? What would *that* look like? (Grown men being told that if they are really serious about becoming Christians, there's a little surgery they need to have . . .)

The first Christians know that Jesus is for everybody, but what do they do with all of these Jewish laws they follow? So they convene a council (*yeshiva* in Hebrew) to discuss it.

After hearing all sides of the issue, they decide to forbid (or should we say they bind?) several things.[17]

Here is why this is so important: They have to make decisions about what it means to be a Christian.

They actually do it. They gather together and make interpretations of the Bible regarding what it will look like for millions of people to be Christians.

I wonder if one of them stood up at any point and said, "Jesus gave us the authority to do this, didn't he?"

Now let's move things into our world. If we take Jesus seriously and actually see it as our responsibility to bind and loose, the implications are endless, serious, and exhilarating.

The Bible is a communal book. It came from people writing in communities, and it was often written to communities. Remember that the printing press wasn't invented until the 1400s. Prior to that, very few if any people had their own copies of the Bible. In Jesus's day, an entire village could probably afford only one copy of the scriptures, if that. Reading the Bible alone was unheard of, if people could even read. For most of church history, people heard the Bible read aloud in a room full of people. You heard it, discussed it, studied it, argued about it, and made decisions about it as a group, a community. Most of the "yous" in the Bible are plural. Groups of people receiving these words. So if one person went off the deep end with an interpretation or opinion, the others were right there to keep that person in check. In a synagogue, most of the people knew the text by heart. When someone got up to teach or share insight, chances are everybody knew the text that person was talking on and already had their own opinions about it. You saw yourself and those around you as taking part in a huge discussion that has gone on for thousands of years.

Because God has spoken, and everything else is commentary.

Contrast this communal way of reading and discussing and learning with our Western, highly individualized culture. In many Christian settings, people are even encouraged to read the Bible alone, which is a new idea in church history. A great idea and a life-changing discipline, but a new idea. And think of pastors. Many pastors study alone all week, stand alone in front of the church and talk about the Bible, and then receive mail and phone calls from individuals who agree or don't agree with what they said. This works for a lot of communities, but it isn't the only way.

And it can't be the only way if we take seriously Jesus's call to be binding and loosing, which must be done in community. In fact, binding and loosing can only be done in community with others who are equally passionate about being true to the words of God.

In Jesus's world, it was assumed that you had as much to learn from the discussion of the text as you did from the text itself. One person could never get too far in a twisted interpretation because the others were right there giving her insight and perspective she didn't have on her own. Jesus said when he was talking about binding and loosing that "where two or three come together in my name, there am I with them."[18]

Community, community, community. Together, with others, wrestling and searching and engaging the Bible as a group of people hungry to know God in order to follow God.

Perhaps this is why the Bible can be confusing for some the first time they read it. I don't think any of the writers of the Bible ever intended people to read their letters alone. I think they assumed that people who were hearing these words for the first time would be sitting next to someone who was further along on her spiritual journey, someone who was more in tune with what the writer was saying. If it didn't make sense, you could stop the person who was reading and say, "Help me understand this."

When we're serious about dealing with the Bible as the communal book that it is, then we have to be honest about our interpretations. Everybody's interpretation is essentially his or her own opinion. Nobody is objective.

Several years ago I was in an intense meeting with our church's leaders in which we were discussing several passages in the Bible. One of the leaders was sharing her journey in trying to understand what the Bible teaches about the issue at hand and said something like this: "I've spent a great deal of time recently studying this issue. I've read what the people on the one side of the issue say, and I've read what the people on the other side say. I've read the scholars and the theologians and all sorts of others on this subject. But then, in the end, I decided to get back to the Bible and just take it for what it really says."

What was she really saying?

Now please understand that this way of thinking is prevalent in a lot of Christian churches, so I don't mean in any way to single her out. But this view of the Bible is warped and toxic, to say the least. The assumption is that there is a way to read the Bible that is agenda- and perspective-free. As if all these other people have their opinion and biases, but some are able to just read it for what it says.

Think about that for a moment: This perspective is claiming that a person can simply read the Bible and do what it says—unaffected by any outside influences.

But let's be honest. When you hear people say they are just going to tell you what the Bible means, it is not true. They are telling you what they *think* it means. They are giving their opinions about the Bible. It sounds nice to say, "I'm not giving you my opinion; I'm just telling you what it means."

The problem is, it is not true.

I'm actually giving you my opinion, my *interpretation* of what it says. And the more I insist that I am giving you the objective truth of what it really says, the less objective I am actually being.

Obviously we think *our* interpretations are the most correct; otherwise we'd change them.

Or as one of my favorite writers, Anne Lamott, put it, "Everybody thinks their opinion is the right one. If they didn't, they'd get a new one."[19]

The idea that everybody else approaches the Bible with baggage and agendas and lenses and I don't is the ultimate in arrogance. To think that I can just read the Bible without reading any of my own culture or background or issues into it and come out with a "pure" or "exact" meaning is not only untrue, but it leads to a very destructive reading of the Bible that robs it of its life and energy.

I have heard people say their church is growing because they "just teach the Bible." As if other churches don't. And what about the church that teaches the Bible and shrinks? The church that's growing in numbers is probably growing for a lot of reasons, but the teaching-the-Bible reason is that they are teaching a particular understanding of the Bible. A yoke. They aren't objective, and they aren't just telling people what it says. They have interpreted it and made decisions about it, and this particular yoke they're spreading resonates with people. This version—their version—is striking a chord with people, and so they are coming to hear more of *this* take on the Bible.

The Bible has to be interpreted. Decisions have to be made about what it means now, today.

The Bible is always coming through the interpretation of someone. And that's because binding and loosing require awareness.

Awareness that everybody's understanding of the Bible rests on *somebody's* binding and loosing.

When was the last time you saw a Christian greet another Christian with a holy kiss? But it's right there in the Bible. I can show you verses in Corinthians and Thessalonians and in one of Peter's letters that say we should greet each other with a holy kiss.[20]

Or how about women having to wear head coverings?[21]
Or cursing people who don't love the Lord?[22]
Or selling all your possessions and giving everything to the poor?[23]
Or men raising their hands when they pray?[24]
Or slaves having to obey their masters?[25]

These are all commands that appear in the Bible. And yet they are rarely followed. This is because someone somewhere made a decision about those texts; someone decided that Christians didn't have to greet one another with a kiss or wear head coverings or curse people who don't love the Lord.

All of these verses have been interpreted by someone, whether it was a priest or a denomination or a pastor or a council somewhere—somebody somewhere engaged in the difficult work of binding and loosing. Somebody in your history decided certain Bible verses still apply and others don't.

At one point in church history, a group of Christians decided that the Sabbath is not Saturday but Sunday. If you go to a mass or service or house church on Sunday, then you are, in essence, agreeing with their binding and loosing.

Now some people may get a little uneasy about this discussion on interpreting the Bible and say, "We shouldn't make it say what we want it to say."

I agree, but everybody is resting on a set of interpretations, and we need to be honest about it.

And not only is everybody resting on someone's binding and loosing, but that binding and loosing was new for its day. When people stepped forward and said, "You have heard it interpreted this way, but I tell you it really means this," it was progressive for their day. They were making new claims about what it means to be true to the Bible. What is accepted today as tradition was at one point in time a break from tradition.

This truth about interpreting the Bible extends all the way to the simple reading of it in English. If we don't read the Bible in its original Greek or Hebrew or Aramaic, then we are reading someone's interpretation of the Bible. Just the work of translating requires the translator to make decisions about what the Bible says. Certain Greek or Hebrew or Aramaic words do not have an exact English equivalent, leaving the translator with a challenge of how to best represent the text using English words.

Here's an example: The word *hell* is found fourteen times in the Bible, twelve of those occurrences being found in the teachings of Jesus. The word *hell* in English is the word *gehenna* in Greek. Gehenna is a reference to the Valley of Hinnom, a ravine on the south side of the city of Jerusalem. This valley was the site over the years of many violent and horrible deaths, and it came to be viewed as cursed. By Jesus's day it had become the town dump. Garbage, trash, wild animals fighting over scraps of food, a fire burning—a place of waste and destruction. Some referred to it as the place with the gnashing of teeth where the fire never dies. So when Jesus uses *gehenna*, it is loaded with meaning and visual power—everybody knew what he was talking about. The translator is faced with a decision about how to translate the word. If he or she uses the word *hell,* later readers might miss the fact that Jesus is talking about a present reality. If the word *gehenna* is used, readers might understand the present, geographical meaning of the word but miss the bigger implications. Every translation, every version, every paraphrase of the Bible requires thousands of decisions about how to interpret what these words are saying to us today.

Which leads to another observation: Binding and loosing demand an intricate balance of conviction and humility.

When those first Christians in Acts 15 came out of their meeting and announced their decision regarding the Gentiles, they said the strangest thing: "It seemed good to the Holy Spirit and to us not to burden you with anything beyond the following requirements."[26]

Let me repeat that one phrase again: "It *seemed* good to the Holy Spirit and to us."

They are making a monumental decision in the history of Christianity, and the best they can say is that it *seems* like it is the best decision? It seems good to them and the Holy Spirit?

They don't claim to have an absolute word from God on the matter; they at best claim guidance from the Spirit of God, but they even hold that loosely.

What is so beautiful about the language in Acts 15 is that they make a decision, they step up, they take their responsibility seriously, they acknowledge a strong sense of God's leading, but they remain humble.

With their "seems," they leave room to admit they may not have nailed it perfectly the first time. They hold their action and God's action in healthy tension. They understand that they have action to take, but they also understand that God is at work as well. They don't take a passive route, which is to do nothing and assume that God will miraculously do it all. And they don't take a route based in human arrogance, which leaves no room for the leading and guiding of the Spirit of God.

What if we were to say about what we do, "It seems good to the Holy Spirit and to us"?

I love the sense of movement in these first Christians' language, like they are discovering things and making decisions, but there is this inherent assumption that they are on a journey. There is more ahead. And God is with them every step of the way.

They aren't done painting.

Alive Today

Here's another observation about binding and loosing: You can only bind and loose if you believe the Bible is alive.

Let me get at this truth with a question: Is the greatest truth about Adam and Eve and the fruit that it *happened,* or that it *happens*?[27] This story, one of the first in the Bible, is true for us because it is our story. We have all taken the fruit. We have all crossed boundaries. We have all made decisions to do things our way and then looked back and said to ourselves, *What was I thinking?* The fruit looked so great to Adam and Eve for those brief moments, but the consequences were with them for the rest of their lives. Their story is our story. We see ourselves in them. The story is true for us because it happened and because it *happens.* It is an accurate description of how life is. The reason the stories in the Bible have resonated with so many people over the years is that they have seen themselves in these stories.

Here is another example: The Israelites leave the kingdom of Egypt where they are slaves, and God brings them out into freedom.

It happens.
Every day.

For many of us, that is our story. We were in darkness and God brought us out. And we continue to identify areas of darkness in our lives, and God continues to bring us out.

So the exodus is the Israelites' story, but it is also our story. It happened then; it happens now.

In fact, in a Jewish synagogue to this day, you will probably hear kids taught the story of Exodus as their story. A friend of mine recently heard a Jewish kid say, "*We* were slaves in Egypt and Moses led us out, and *we* complained in the wilderness."

This is why the Bible is still so powerful: These ancient stories are *our* stories. These stories are reflective of how things are.

And this is why the Bible loses its power for so many communities. They fall into the trap of thinking that the Bible is just about things that happened a long time ago.

But the Bible is about today.

These stories are our stories. They are alive and active and teaching us about our lives in our world, today.

The rabbis spoke of the text being like a gem with seventy faces, and each time you turn the gem, the light refracts differently, giving you a reflection you haven't seen before. And so we turn the text again and again because we keep seeing things we missed the time before.[28]

I was talking to a pastor several years ago who was preparing a sermon, and I asked him if he was ready to give it. He said, "Oh yeah, I've got this passage nailed." How is that possible?

When you embrace the text as living and active, when you enter into its story, when you keep turning the gem, you never come to the end.

I just wrote a phrase from the Bible on the wall of the room I am writing in right now. It's from John 11 where a man named Lazarus dies. Jesus meets up with Lazarus's sisters who are complaining that Jesus got there too late to save their brother. When Jesus tells them to roll away the stone in front of where Lazarus is buried, one of the sisters, Martha, complains that there will be a terrible odor, "for he has been there four days."[29]

The King James Version reads like this: "He stinketh."

For some odd reason, I have not been able to get that phrase out of my head lately. "He stinketh." It's working on me. It's teaching me. I've been meditating and reflecting on it and turning it over and over in my head and my heart. Inspired words have a way of getting under our skin and taking on a life of their own. They work on us. We started out reading them, but they end up reading us.

This is what happens when the Bible becomes living and active. The strangest dimensions of these stories grab us and won't let go.

And this phrase continues to swirl around in my mind and my heart. Where is there death in my life? Where am I dying because of decisions I've made? Where do I "stinketh"?

"He stinketh" is written on the wall of this room because it is my story.

It happened in John 11.
It happens for me every day.

The reason the Bible continues to resonate with so many people isn't just because it happened. What gives us strength and meaning and direction is something in addition to the historical events: It is the meaning of these events. Some call this the more-than-literal truth of the Bible.[30]

We live in the metaphors. The story of David and Goliath continues to speak to us because we know the David part of the story—we have lived it. The tomb is empty because we have met the risen Christ—we have experienced Jesus in a way that transcends space and time. And this gives us hope. We were in darkness and God brought us out into the light.

The Word is living and active and it happens. Today.

Real, Real, Real

In order to bind and loose, we must understand that the Bible did not drop out of the sky. It was written by people. People who told stories and passed on oral traditions and sat down and wrote things with a pen and paper. The Bible originated from real people in real places at real times.

It is poems and stories and letters and accounts. It is people interacting with other people in actual space and time. It is God interacting with people in actual space and time. We cannot ignore this.

To take statements made in a letter from one person living in a real place at a moment in history writing to another person living in a real place out of their context and apply them to today without first understanding their original context sucks the life right out of them. They aren't isolated statements that float, unattached, out in space.

They aren't first and foremost timeless truths.

We may, and usually do, find timeless truths present in the Bible, but it is because they were true in real places for real people at real times.

I heard somebody recently refer to the Bible as "data." That person was in an intense discussion about what the Bible teaches about a certain issue, and he disagreed with someone else so he said, "I don't see the data for your position."

Data?

The Bible is not pieces of information about God and Jesus and whatever else we take and apply to situations as we would a cookbook or an instruction manual.

And while I'm at it, let's make a group decision to drop once and for all the Bible-as-owner's-manual metaphor. It's terrible. It really is.

When was the last time you read the owner's manual for your toaster? Do you find it remotely inspiring or meaningful?

You only refer to it when something's wrong with your toaster. You use it to fix the problem, and then you put it away.

We have to embrace the Bible as the wild, uncensored, passionate account it is of people experiencing the living God.

Doubting the one true God.

Wrestling with, arguing with, getting angry with, reconciling with, loving, worshipping, thanking, following the one who gives us everything.

We cannot tame it.
We cannot tone it down.

If we do, then we can't say it is the life-giving Word of God. We have made it something else.

So when we treat the Bible as if it floats in space, unattached to when and where it actually happened, we are basically saying that God gave us the wrong kind of book. It is a book of ancient narratives. We cannot make it something it is not.[31]

When Jesus talks about divorce, he is entering into a discussion that was one of the eight great debates of his day.[32] He is interacting with a specific tradition and other rabbis of his day who had said specific things about divorce. The great rabbis Hillel and Shammai had specific yokes in regard to divorce. When Jesus is asked questions about divorce, what he is really being asked is, "Who do you side with, Hillel or Shammai?" People are asking him to enter into the current discussion. And in Jesus's answer, he sides with one of them.[33] To grab a few lines of Jesus and drop them down on someone 2,000 years later without first entering into the world in which they first appeared is lethal to the life and vitality and *truth* of the Bible.

Real people, in real places, at real times, writing and telling stories about their experiences and their growing understanding of who God is and who they are.

This does not in any way discount the power of reading the Bible with no background knowledge at all, which is why these words are so powerful. We can enter into them at any level and they speak to us. Whether we are reading the Bible for the first time or standing in a field in Israel next to a historian and an archaeologist and a scholar, the Bible meets us where we are. That is what truth does.

For example, the book of Deuteronomy is patterned after treaties that were common in its day. The writer essentially took a common legal document and changed the content and the names but kept the form the same.

The end of the book of Mark is arranged according to the coronation ceremonies of the Roman emperor. Maybe Mark witnessed one of these ceremonies, because he is very intentional about the order of events leading up to Jesus's death. His readers would have been familiar with these Roman coronation events. They would have read between the lines right away. Mark wants you to see Jesus as a king like Caesar, but at the same time totally unlike Caesar.

The first three miracles in the book of John are directly related to the three major gods of Asia Minor, the region John writes his gospel to. Dionysus was the god who turned water into wine, Asclepius was the god of healing, and Demeter was the goddess of grain. So how does John begin his story? With Jesus turning water into wine, healing, and then feeding thousands of people. John has an agenda. He wants these people in this place and this time to know that Jesus is better than their gods.

When Paul writes to Timothy about women being saved in childbirth, he is making a direct reference to the goddess Artemis, whose temple was just down the street in Timothy's hometown of Ephesus. Artemis's followers believed that Artemis saved women from dying in childbirth, which is significant in a city where one out of two women died giving birth. Paul's statement here has huge political, social, and religious implications. He is implying that Artemis is a fraud.[34]

The first chapters of the book of Revelation follow the sequence of events of the Domitian games, held in honor of the caesar who was in power at the time Revelation was written. Domitian would address the leaders of the various provinces, then his choir of twenty-four would sing worship songs to him, and then there would be a horse race. John is writing Revelation to people who had seen the Domitian games; they know exactly what he is referring to. He wants them to see that Domitian is a fake and Jesus is the real King.

The writers of the Bible are communicating in language their world will understand. They are using the symbols and pictures and images of the culture they are speaking to. That's why the Bible has authority—God has authority and is present in real space and time. The Bible is a collection of stories that teach us about what it looks like when God is at work *through actual people.* The Bible has the authority it does only because it contains stories about people interacting with the God who has all authority.

The point in the book of Acts isn't the early church. The point is the God who is at work in and through the early church to change the world.[35] When we take the Bible seriously, we are taking God seriously. We believe that the same God who was at work then is at work now. The same God in the same kinds of ways. The goal is not to be a "New Testament church." That makes the New Testament church the authority. The authority is God who is acting in and through those people at that time and now these people at this time.

The point is to ask, what is God up to here, now?
What in the world is God doing today?
How should we respond?
How did they respond?
What can we learn from them that will help us now?

This is why binding and loosing is so exhilarating. You can only do it if you believe and see God at work now, here in this place. You are reacting to a God who is alive and well and working and saving and redeeming.

The Bible tells a story. A story that isn't over. A story that is still being told. A story that we have a part to play in.

Creating and Recognizing

In order to bind and loose, we have to think about inspiration in terms of recognition as well as creation. Here's what I mean: People sat down and wrote things on paper. Well, sometimes even that came a lot later. Much of the Bible was oral tradition that was circulating for years and years before someone wrote it down.

Picture a campfire thousands of years ago in what is Iraq today. A group of shepherds have gathered at the end of the day; the meal is over and the stories begin to flow, and a young girl says to her uncle, "Tell me again why the world is how it is."

And her uncle responds: "In the beginning God created . . ."

Back to the writing part. The people who eventually wrote all of this down weren't sitting there with their hand and the pen moving as if controlled by some outside force.

The writers of the Bible had agendas.
Luke said he wrote to give an orderly account of all that has gone down.
John said he wrote so we will believe in Jesus.
The writer of the book of Ruth had some strong opinions about Jews marrying Gentiles.

The writers obviously took what they were doing very seriously and had specific outcomes they wanted from their writings, but that doesn't mean they woke up in the morning thinking, *Today I'll write a section of the Bible.*

Now, apparently their writings were recognized as inspired soon after their creation. Peter mentions the writings of Paul in one of his letters: "[Paul] writes the same way in all his letters, speaking in them of these matters. His letters contain some things that are hard to understand, which ignorant and unstable people distort, as they do the other scriptures, to their own destruction."[36]

I love that phrase "hard to understand." The Bible was difficult to grasp on the first pass for people who had written it.

But my point here is that Peter is referring to the writings of Paul in the same light as "the other scriptures."

Already early in the life of the Jesus movement, certain letters and writings were beginning to distinguish themselves as being different, inspired, "from God" in ways that other religious writings weren't. For the next several hundred years, there was a lot of discussion in the Christian community about which books were considered scripture and which books weren't. But it wasn't until the 300s that what we know as the sixty-six books of the Bible were actually agreed upon as "the Bible."

This is part of the problem with continually insisting that one of the absolutes of the Christian faith must be a belief that "scripture alone" is our guide. It sounds nice, but it is not true.[37] In reaction to abuses by the church, a group of believers during a time called the Reformation claimed that we only need the authority of the Bible. But the problem is that we got the Bible from the church voting on what the Bible even is. So when I affirm the Bible as God's Word, in the same breath I have to affirm that when those people voted, God was somehow present, guiding them to do what they did. When people say that all we need is the Bible, it is simply not true.

In affirming the Bible as inspired, I have to affirm the Spirit who I believe was inspiring those people to choose those books.[38]

Were they binding and loosing the Bible itself?

At some point we have to have faith. Faith that God is capable of guiding people. Faith that God has not left us alone. Faith that the same Spirit who guided Paul and Peter and those people in a room in the 300s is still

with
us
today.

Guiding us, showing us, enlightening us.

Wrestling

Binding and loosing can only be done if communities are willing to wrestle. The ultimate display of our respect for the sacred words of God is that we are willing to wade in and struggle with the text—the good parts, the hard-to-understand parts, the parts we wish weren't there.

The rabbis even say a specific blessing when they don't understand a portion of the text. When it eludes them, when it makes no sense, they say a word of thanks to God because of the blessing that will be theirs someday. "Thank you, God, that at some point in the future, the lights are going to come on for me."

The rabbis have a metaphor for this wrestling with the text: The story of Jacob wrestling the angel in Genesis 32. He struggles, and it is exhausting and tiring, and in the end his hip is injured. It hurts. And he walks away limping.

Because when you wrestle with the text, you walk away limping.

And some people have no limp, because they haven't wrestled. But the ones limping have had an experience with the living God.

I think God does know what he's doing with the Bible. But a better question is, do *we* know what *we're* doing with the Bible?

And I say, yes, we are binding and loosing and wrestling and limping.

Because God has spoken.

MOVEMENT THREE

TRUE

I remember the first time I was truly in awe of God. I was caught up for the first time in my life in something so massive and loving and transcendent and . . . true. Something I was sure could be trusted. I specifically remember thinking the universe was safe, in spite of all the horrible, tragic things in the world. I remember being overwhelmed with the word *true*. Underneath it all life is somehow . . . good . . . and I was sixteen and at a U2 concert. The Joshua Tree tour. When they started with the song "Where the Streets Have No Name," I thought I was going to spontaneously combust with joy. This was real. This mattered. Whatever it was, I wanted more.

I had never felt that way before.

I remember surfing Trestles—the legendary beach between Los Angeles and San Diego—for the first time. I paddled out on a gorgeous day, and as I sat there on my board, a couple hundred feet off shore, surrounded by blue and green and sunlight and quiet, a dolphin jumped in the water next to me. I thought my heart was never going to start beating again. Beauty can be crushing at times, can't it?

I remember when my first son was born and I couldn't speak. Which for those who know me well was an act of God in itself, perhaps equal to the birth of a child. I will never forget standing there by the bed and hearing the doctor ask me what my son's name was and being unable to answer. I just couldn't answer. I tried so hard, but I couldn't get the words out. I couldn't get anything out.

What I find fascinating is how many of us have had moments like these when we were overwhelmed with the presence of something or somebody so—and it is hard to find words here—so good, so right, so true, so safe.

Warmth, comfort, terror—but the good kind of terror. Maybe we should say "awe." You have your own ways of describing these moments.

Some friends of mine just returned from Haiti where they spent a week holding babies in an orphanage. They are still trying to find words.

But it isn't just extraordinary experiences when this happens, is it? It also happens in the day-to-day, ordinary moments. I was with my friends at one of our favorite restaurants the other night. We had been there at least three hours when I noticed we were the last ones in the place. The employees were starting to stack chairs and vacuum the floors, and we were still talking. I was looking around the table at my wife, whom I just adore; our friend Shauna, who may be one of the best storytellers on the planet; Tom, whom I would take a bullet for; and Tom's wife, Cecilia, who is one of the most loving, authentic people I have ever met. And I'm sitting in this restaurant looking around the table, soaking it in, totally over-whelmed with the holiness of it all. The sacredness of the moment. That sense that in spite of everything awful I have ever seen, we're going to make it. I know that sounds like it's from a greeting card, but I know you know what I'm talking about. Ordinary moments in ordinary settings that all of a sudden become infused with some-thing else. With meaning. Significance. Hope.

The neighbor kids, Malcolm and Isabel, were over a few nights ago with their dad, Tim. My boys got out plastic sleds, and we were trying to see who could sled down the hill in our front yard . . . in September. Cars were slowing down as they drove by, filled with people wondering if these kids were actually sledding on grass. And I was standing in the front yard laughing and pushing the kids down the hill. The trees overhead were just starting to turn color, and Tim was telling a bizarre story about what had happened to him that day, and the kids were laughing, and everything was in its right place.

I assume you have had moments like this when you were caught up in something so much bigger than yourself that you couldn't even put it in words.

What is it about certain things that ignite something within?

And is that *something* actually *someone*?

Whatever those things are that make you feel fully alive and like the universe is ultimately a good place and you are not alone, I need a faith that doesn't deny these moments but embraces them. I need a spiritual under-standing that celebrates these kinds of transcendent moments instead of avoiding them. These moments can't be tangents. They can't be experiences that distract from "real" faith. These moments can't exist on the edges, because they are a part of our faith. A spirituality that is real will have to make sense of them and show us how they fit. They are expressions of what it means to live in God's world.

Something Bigger

I was in Rwanda a few years ago, and a group of us went hiking in the slums of Kigali with a woman named Pauline. Pauline spends her free time caring for people who are about to die of HIV/AIDS. She agreed to take us to visit one of her friends who had only hours to live. We hiked through this slum for what seemed like miles, and as we got farther in, the shacks became smaller and smaller until all we had to walk on were narrow trails with sewage crisscrossing in streams that ran beside, and sometimes under, the shacks.

Eventually we ended up in a dirt-floored, one-room shack about six-by-six feet. A woman was lying under so many blankets that all we could see was her mouth and eyes. Her name was Jacqueline. Pauline had become her friend and had been visiting her consistently for the past few months. As I knelt down beside her on the floor, I watched Pauline, standing in the corner, weeping. Her friend was going to die soon. What overwhelmed me wasn't the death or despair or poverty. What overwhelmed me was the compassion. In this dark place Pauline's love and compassion were simply . . . bigger. More. It is as if the smallest amount of light is infinitely more powerful than massive amounts of dark. The ground was holy.

I'm sure you have had similar experiences. In the strangest of settings, maybe with people you barely know, you become aware that the ground beneath your feet is holy. It is sacred. There's something else, something *more,* going on here.

I went to a funeral several years ago and walked into the lobby of the chapel and immediately thought I was the first one there. Then I realized I wasn't the first one; the husband of the woman who had died was there, standing over the open casket. I walked over to him as he stood over her body, put my arm around him, and didn't say anything. Just the two of us in this big open room, looking down at his wife's body. He just kept saying over and over, "She was such a good woman; she was such a good woman." And we stood there together for a while with my arm around his shoulder, and I listened to him repeat, "She was such a good woman." The ground was holy.

A young woman in our church gave birth last week to a two-pound baby who died the day after being born. My friend Matt went to the hospital to visit them. When he entered the room, he realized the baby was still there. And the couple was sitting in shock, stunned that this had happened and happened to them. Matt walked in, greeted the couple, and then took the baby in his arms and kissed it.

I wasn't even there, and I can feel the moment. The pain, the anguish, the sense that something else was going on in that room that we only get glimpses of from time to time.

Because it isn't just concerts and surfing and the high points, and it isn't just those beautiful moments in the midst of the everyday and mundane; it is also in the tragic and the gut-wrenching moments when we cannot escape the simple fact that there is way more going on around us than we realize.

Everywhere

Last year some friends asked me to be the pastor for their wedding ceremony. They had been together for a while and decided to make it official and throw a huge weekend party, and they invited me to be a part of it. They said they didn't want any Jesus or God or Bible or religion to be talked about. But they did want me to make it really spiritual. The bride said it in her own great way, "Rob, do that thing you do. Make it really profound and deep and spiritual!"

So we decided to meet the morning of the wedding to actually plan the ceremony. It was a stunningly beautiful day, and we met on a cliff overlooking a lake in the midst of a thick forest. The wind was blowing the tops of the trees way up above us, the sun was coming through in yellow-and-white beams, and at one point an eagle flew overhead. I kept waiting for someone to cue the orchestra.

Anyway, I asked my friends why they wanted to be married in such a natural, organic setting, since it was four hours from where we all live. They talked about the beauty of nature, its peacefulness, and the way they fell in love in this part of the state. Then the groom said something I will never forget: "Something holds this all together."

Something holds this all together.

So then I asked them if they thought it was a mistake that they had found each other. And they said, no, they believed they were meant to be together and it was no accident that they met and fell in love. I then asked them, "Do you think whatever it is that holds all *this* together is the same thing that has brought you two together?" They said yes. Same thing.

So I said that maybe what makes their relationship so meaningful to them is that it's a picture of something much bigger. The same force that brought them together holds the whole world together. I then asked, "So today, your wedding is about something far more significant than just the two of you becoming husband and wife, isn't it?"

They then said they would call this glue, this force, "God."

I tell you all this to point out that my friends already intuitively believe certain things about the universe and the way the world works. All I was doing was asking questions about things they already knew to be true.

I didn't have to convince them of anything. Now I could go on about the ceremony and the party afterward and the way it ended up being one of the most sacred things I have ever been a part of, but I want to leave you up on that cliff having that conversation.

The ancient Jewish prophets had these same kinds of spiritual experiences that we do, and they had the same sense that something holds it all together. The prophet Isaiah had a vision of heaven, and in his vision angels were shouting, "Holy, holy, holy, is the Lord Almighty; the whole earth is full of his glory."[1]

The Hebrew word for *glory* here is *kavod,* which means weight or significance.

The whole earth is full of the weight and significance of who God is. The prophets were deeply influenced by this understanding that the earth is drenched with the presence of God.

The writer David said, "The earth is the Lord's, and everything in it."[2]

He later prayed, "Where can I go from your Spirit? Where can I flee from your presence?"[3]

According to the ancient Jewish worldview, God is not somewhere else. God is right here. It is God's world and God made it and God owns it and God is present everywhere in it. In the book of Genesis, a man named Jacob had a dream in which God spoke to him and reminded him of his destiny and purpose. When Jacob woke up, he said, "Surely the Lord is in this place, and I was not aware of it."[4]

God has been there all along, and Jacob is just beginning to realize it. He's waking up from physical sleep, but he is also waking up from spiritual sleep. I've heard people tell stories about something powerful that happened and then at the end of the story say, "And then God showed up!" As if God were somewhere else and then decided to intervene.

But God is always present. We're the ones who show up.

For the ancient Jew, the world is soaked in the presence of God.

The whole earth is full of the *kavod* of God.

For the writers of the Bible, this truth is everywhere. It's here. It's there. It's all over.

And not only is truth everywhere, not only is the whole earth filled with the *kavod* of God, but the writer Paul makes a fascinating observation about people in his letter to the Romans. He says at one point, "Indeed, when Gentiles, who do not have the law, do by nature things required by the law, they are a law for themselves."[5] *Gentiles* is his word for people who don't follow God, and *law* is his word for the scriptures. So he says that people who don't know anything about God are able to do the right thing on a regular basis. Without having any instructions from God or the Bible, these people are still able from time to time to live as God created us to live. For Paul, truth is available to everyone.

Truth is everywhere, and it is available to everyone.

But Paul takes it further, because for him truth is bigger than his religion. Notice what he says in the book of Titus. He is referring to the people who live on the island of Crete when he writes that even one of their own prophets has said, "'Cretans are always liars, evil brutes, lazy gluttons.' He has surely told the truth."[6]

So Paul quotes one of the Cretan prophets and then affirms that this guy was right in what he said. "This testimony is true." What the prophet said was true, so Paul quotes him. For Paul, anybody is capable of speaking truth. Anybody, from any perspective, from any religion, from anywhere.

And these words from the book of Titus, the quote from a Cretan prophet, are in the Bible. So the Word of God contains the words of a prophet from Crete.

Paul affirms the truth wherever he finds it.

But he takes it further in the book of Acts. He is speaking at a place called Mars Hill (which would be a great name for a church) and trying to explain to a group of people who believe in hundreds of thousands of gods that there is really only one God who made everything and everybody. At one point he's talking about how God made us all, and he says to them, "As some of your own poets have said, 'We are his offspring.'"[7] He quotes their own poets. And their poets don't even believe in the God he's talking about. They were talking about some other god and how we are all the offspring of that god, and Paul takes their statement and makes it about his God. Amazing.

Paul doesn't just affirm the truth here; he claims it for himself. He doesn't care who said it or who they were even saying it about. What they said was true, and so he claims it as his own.

This affirming and claiming of truth wherever you find it is all through the writings of Paul. In 1 Corinthians, he tells his readers, "All things are yours, . . . and you are of Christ, and Christ is of God."[8] He essentially says to them, "It all belongs to God, and Christ is of God, and you are of Christ, so . . . it's all yours."

Claim it.

If it is true, if it is beautiful, if it is honorable, if it is right, then claim it. Because it is from God. And you belong to God.

The philosopher Arthur Holmes is known for saying, "All truth is God's truth." It is such a great statement, because what other kind of truth could there be?

So as a Christian, I am free to claim the good, the true, the holy, *wherever* and *whenever* I find it. I live with the understanding that truth is bigger than any religion and the world is God's and everything in it.

I was traveling in Turkey awhile back and kept noticing that a large number of the homes there seemed unfinished. Piles of wood and brick beside the house, half a foundation built, construction equipment everywhere. It looked like a lot of homes had been started and then the workers went to lunch . . . for a year. I asked my friend, who has spent a lot of time in Turkey, about it. He said the reason is that the Muslim culture doesn't allow for financial debt, so people only build with cash. They work for a while, run out of money, save up, keep working, and eventually get the house done, which they own, debt-free. I was struck with how different Western culture would be if we had a similar aversion to debt. How many people do we know who are crippled with financial debt? Having less debt is a better way to live. I affirm this value of the Muslim people of Turkey because it is true, it is good, and it is a better way to live. It doesn't matter where I find it, who speaks or lives it, or what they believe, I claim and affirm the truth wherever I find it.

All things are mine.

Why would we ever be surprised when truth turns up in strange places?

Logos

Do you know anybody who grew up in a religious environment, maybe even a Christian one, and walked away from faith/church/God when they turned eighteen and went away to college?

Whenever I ask this question in a group of people, almost every hand goes up. Let me suggest why. Imagine what happens when a young woman is raised in a Christian setting but hasn't been taught that all things are hers and then goes to a university where she's exposed to all sorts of new ideas and views and perspectives. She takes classes in psychology and anthropology and biology and world history, and her professors are people who have devoted themselves to their particular fields of study. Is it possible that in the course of lecturing on their field of interest, her professors will from time to time say things that are true? Of course. Truth is available to everyone.

But let's say her professors aren't Christians, it is not a "Christian" university, and this young woman hasn't been taught that all things are hers. What if she has been taught that Christianity is the only thing that's true? What if she has been taught that there is no truth outside the Bible? She's now faced with this dilemma: believe the truth she's learning or the Christian faith she was brought up with.

Or we could put her dilemma this way: intellectual honesty or Jesus?

How many times have you seen this? I can't tell you the number of people in their late teens or early twenties I know, or those I have been told about, who experience truth outside the boundaries of their religion and abandon the whole thing because they think it's a choice (which is a fatal flaw in thinking we'll address in a moment). They are experiencing truth in all sorts of new ways, and they need a faith that is big enough to handle it. Their box is getting blown apart, and the faith they were handed doesn't have room for what they are learning.

But it isn't a choice, because Jesus said, "I am the way, the truth, the life." If you come across truth in any form, it isn't outside your faith as a Christian. Your faith just got bigger. To be a Christian is to claim truth wherever you find it.

It's not truth over here and Jesus over there, as if they were two different things. Where we find one, we find the other. Jesus is quoted in the book of John saying, "I and the Father are one." If Jesus and God are one, if Jesus shows us what God is really, truly like, and God is truth and all truth is God's truth, then Jesus takes us into the truth, not away from it. He frees us to embrace whatever is true and good and beautiful wherever we find it.

To live this way then, we have to believe in a big Jesus. For many, Jesus was presented to them as the solution to a problem. In fact, this has been the dominant way of explaining the story of the Bible in Western culture for the past several hundred years. It's not that it is wrong; it's just that Jesus is so much more. The presentation often begins with sin and the condition of human beings, separated from God and without hope in the world. God then came up with a way to fix the problem by sending Jesus, who came to the world to give us a way out of the mess we find ourselves in. So if we were to draw a continuum of the story of the Bible, Jesus essentially shows up late in the game.

But the first Christians didn't see Jesus this way, as if God were somewhere else and then cooked up some way to solve the sin problem at the last minute by getting involved as Jesus. They believed that Jesus was somehow *more,* that Jesus had actually been present since before creation and had been a part of the story all along.

In the first line of his gospel, John calls Jesus the "Word." The word *Word* here in Greek is the word *logos,* which is where we get the English word *logic.*

Logic, intelligence, design. The blueprint of creation.

When we speak of these concepts, what we are describing is the way the world is arranged. There is some sort of order under the chaos, and some people seem to have a better handle on it than others. Some understand math, some the human psyche, and others can speak clearly and compellingly about the solar system. When we say someone is intelligent, we are saying they have insight as to how things are put together.

And the Bible keeps insisting that Jesus is how God put things together. The writer Paul said that Jesus is how God holds all things together.[9] The Bible points us to a Jesus who is in some mysterious way *behind it all.*

Jesus *is* the arrangement. Jesus *is* the design. Jesus *is* the intelligence. For a Christian, Jesus's teachings aren't to be followed because they are a nice way to live a moral life. They are to be followed because they are the best possible insight into how the world really works. They teach us how things are.

I don't follow Jesus because I think Christianity is the best religion. I follow Jesus because he leads me into ultimate reality. He teaches me to live in tune with how reality is. When Jesus said, "No one comes to the Father except through me," he was saying that his way, his words, his life is our connection to how things truly are at the deepest levels of existence.[10] For Jesus then, the point of religion is to help us connect with ultimate reality, God. I love the way Paul puts it in the book of Colossians: These religious acts and rituals are shadows of the reality. "The reality . . . is found in Christ."[11]

Labels

It is dangerous to label things "Christian." The word *Christian* first appears in the Bible as a noun. The first followers of Jesus were called Christians because they had devoted themselves to living the way of the Messiah, who they believed was Jesus.

Noun. A person. A person who follows Jesus. A person living in tune with ultimate reality, God. A way of life centered around a person who lives.

The problem with turning the noun into an adjective and then tacking it onto words is that it can create categories that limit the truth. Here's what I mean: Something can be labeled "Christian" and not be true or good. I was speaking at a pastors' conference several years ago, and a well-known pastor was going to be speaking after me. I thought I'd stick around when I was done because I wanted to hear what he had to say. It was shocking. He essentially told the roomful of pastors that if their churches weren't growing and they weren't happy all the time and they weren't healthy and successful, then they probably weren't "called and chosen by God" to be pastors. I can't imagine the messages his talk put in the hearts and minds of those pastors who were listening. I couldn't begin to understand how he made those verses mean that. And it was a Christian pastor talking in a Christian church to other Christian pastors. But it wasn't true.

This happens in all sorts of areas. It is possible for music to be labeled Christian and be terrible music. It could lack creativity and inspiration. The lyrics could be recycled clichés. That "Christian" band could actually be giving Jesus a bad name because they aren't a great band. It is possible for a movie to be a "Christian" movie and to be a terrible movie. It may actually desecrate the art form in its quality and storytelling and craft. Just because it is a "Christian" book by a "Christian" author and it was purchased in a "Christian" bookstore doesn't mean it is all true or good or beautiful. A "Christian" political group puts me in an awkward position: What if I disagree with them? Am I less of a Christian? What if I am convinced the Christian thing to do is to vote the exact opposite?

Christian is a great noun and a poor adjective.

I was playing in a punk band a few years ago, and we were playing clubs and bars and festivals and parties. People would regularly ask us if we were a Christian band when they found out I was a pastor. I always found the question a bit odd. When you meet a plumber, do you ask her if she is a Christian plumber? I realize now why I chafed against the question.

My understanding is that to be Christian is to do whatever it is that you do with great passion and devotion. We throw ourselves into our work because everything is sacred. I love how Paul put it in Colossians: "Whatever you do, whether in word or deed, do it all in the name of the Lord Jesus."[12] He is teaching people to live as Christians, and then whatever they do will be sacred, holy work. Music already is worship. Music is praise. Music is sacred. Music is good. Creation doesn't need a label to make it sacred or acceptable or blessed. When God made the world, God called it "good." Now obviously anything can be corrupted and desecrated and used for purposes other than those which God intends, but making music is sacred enough. Paul put it like this: "For everything God created is good."[13]

This is why Jesus wouldn't have blessed the food before he ate. He blessed God for providing the earth, which provides the food. The food is already blessed, because it comes from the earth, and "the earth is the Lord's, and everything in it."[14]

This is why it is impossible for a Christian to have a secular job. If you follow Jesus and you are doing what you do in his name, then it is no longer secular work; it's sacred. You are there; God is there. The difference is our awareness.

This truth has significant implications for how churches function.

Somebody asked me the other day why our church doesn't support the arts because we don't have dramas and short-act plays in the services. I realized the question, as with almost every question, goes back to creation. I don't believe something has to be in a church service to be "for God." As if the only acting that is "for God" is acting in a church service. A church is a community of people who are learning how to be certain kinds of people wherever they find themselves, so they can do whatever it is they do "in the name of the Lord Jesus." The goal isn't to bring everyone's work into the church; the goal is for the church to be these unique kinds of people who are transforming the places they live and work and play because they understand the whole earth is filled with the *kavod* of God. God isn't in one building only. Doing things for God happens all the time, everywhere. If you are an actor, the goal isn't for you to do your work in a church building in a church service. Please go wherever it is in the world that people act and do it well. Really well. Throw yourself into it and give it everything you have.

So the labels ultimately fail, no matter how useful they are from time to time, because the life of Jesus is just that, a life that is lived by people who have oriented their entire lives around being true to Jesus's teachings.

One of the first things God does in creating the world is separate dark and light. The ancient rabbis say the first thing God does is distinguish between dark and light, and the rest of the scriptures is God teaching people how to distinguish between dark and light. Huge sections of the book of Leviticus are devoted to God teaching people how to discern between life and death, light and dark, clean and unclean. The Ten Commandments are God teaching people how to discern, and how to live well in relationship between right and wrong with their creator. The Bible is filled with stories of God teaching people how to think. How to discern. How to sort and sift and figure out what is true and what isn't. What is good and what isn't. What brings life and what brings death.

Being a Christian is about engaging the mind and heart more and more, not shutting them off or letting someone else think for you. The writer Peter urged Christians to be alert.[15] Paul tells his listeners in Thessalonica to test everything and hold on to the good.[16]

The danger of labeling things "Christian" is that it can lead to our blindly consuming things we have been told are safe and acceptable. When we turn off this discernment radar, dangerous things can happen. We have to test everything. I thank God for the many Christians who create and write and film and sing. Anybody anywhere who is doing all they can to point people to the deeper realities of God is doing a beautiful thing. But those writers and artists and thinkers and singers would all tell you to think long and hard about what they are saying and doing and creating. Test it. Probe it.

Do that to this book. Don't swallow it uncritically. Think about it. Wrestle with it. Just because I'm a Christian and I'm trying to articulate a Christian worldview doesn't mean I've got it nailed. I'm contributing to the discussion. God has spoken, and the rest is commentary, right?

Tour Guides

In the same way that something can be labeled "Christian" and not be true, something can be true and not be labeled Christian. Paul quotes Cretan prophets and Greek poets. He is interested in whether or not what they said is true. Now to be able to quote these prophets and poets, Paul obviously had to read them. And study them. And analyze them. And I'm sure he came across all kinds of things in their writings that he didn't agree with. So he sifts and sorts and separates the light from the dark and then claims and quotes the parts that are true.

It is as if Paul is a spiritual tour guide and is taking his readers through their world, pointing out the true and the good wherever he sees it. Notice what he does in the book of Acts. He visits the city of Lystra, which hasn't heard of Jesus or the God Paul believes in, and he tries to figure out how to explain his Christian worldview to them. He tells them, "[God] has not left himself without testimony: He has shown kindness by giving you rain from heaven and crops in their seasons; he provides you with plenty of food and fills your hearts with joy."[17]

Paul essentially asks his audience: Have you had enough food? Who do you think it comes from?

Has it rained so your crops could grow? Who do you think did that?

Have you ever laughed? Who do you think made that possible?

Missions then are less about the transportation of God from one place to another and more about the identification of a God who is already there. It is almost as if being a good missionary means having really good eyesight. Or maybe it means teaching people to use their eyes to see things that have always been there; they just didn't realize it. You see God where others don't. And then you point him out.

Perhaps we ought to replace the word *missionary* with *tour guide,* because we cannot show people something we haven't seen.

Have you ever heard missionaries say they were going to "take Jesus" to a certain place? What they meant, I assume, was that they had Jesus and they were going to take him to a place like China or India or Chicago where people apparently didn't have him.

I would ask them if people in China and India and Chicago are eating and laughing and enjoying things and generally *being held together*? Because if they are, then Jesus, in a way that is difficult to fully articulate, is already present there.

So the issue isn't so much taking Jesus to people who don't have him, but going to a place and pointing out to the people there the creative, life-giving God who is already present in their midst.

It is searching for the things they have already affirmed as real and beautiful and true and then telling them who you believe is the *source* of all that. "I am here to tell you where I think it comes from . . ."

And if you do see yourself carrying God to places, it can be exhausting.

God is really heavy.

Some people actually believe that God is absent from a place until they get there. The problem with this idea is that if God is not there before you get there, then there is no "there" in the first place.

Tour guides are people who see depth and texture and connection where others don't. That is why the best teachers are masters of the obvious. They see the same things that we do, but they are aware of so much more. And when they point it out, it changes the way we see everything.

In the books of Matthew and Mark, Jesus has dinner with a group of religious leaders and a woman crashes the party, pouring expensive perfume on Jesus's head. The people Jesus is eating with are mad. This perfume could have been sold and the money used for all sorts of worthy causes. But Jesus defends her. He says, "She has done a beautiful thing to me."[18] Jesus and his dinner companions experience the exact same event, yet they see it from totally different perspectives. Jesus sees another dimension to the events: For him it is a profoundly moving, spiritual, worshipful experience. He points out the beauty of it. The others miss it. He sees it.

He is a tour guide. Pointing out the holy and sacred that are present, right here, right now.

Our Story

We claim the beautiful and the good and the true wherever we find it, because all things are ours. Several years ago I was hanging around after one of our church services, and a young woman named Yvette walked up to me and told me she had been listening to me for the last few weeks and hated everything I was saying and totally disagreed with my teachings and the whole time she just wanted to stand up on her chair and yell at me.

I immediately liked her.

She went on to say that she was studying witchcraft and was totally opposed to the things she heard me saying.

I responded, "But you keep coming back." And then I told her I was thrilled that she kept returning to our gatherings. I hoped that our community would continue to be a safe place for her to question and study and discuss and hear that God loves her exactly as she is.

The Sunday after 9/11 I talked about the need to forgive people when they wrong us. The word *forgive* in the Greek language actually means "to send away." People hurt us and harm us, and we end up carrying around these debts they owe us wherever we go. To forgive is to refuse to carry those debts anymore. After the teaching,

I walked off the stage and saw Yvette lying facedown on the floor, sobbing. She later told me she had been raped years ago and had been carrying rage and anger around with her that controlled her entire life. She realized she had no hope but to turn all of that bitterness and hurt over to Jesus, who had suffered far more than even her. And while she was at it, she might as well turn her will and her life and everything else over to him.

So I saw her a few months ago, and she handed me a sheet of paper with her email and phone number on it. I asked her what it was for, and she started telling me stories of the women she had been meeting who were witches but wanted to become Christians, and if I met any, to send them to her. And the more she talked, the more excited she got, telling me how she's "an expert in this."[19]

Beautiful, isn't it? I claim Yvette's story. And you should too. Her story is our story. And our story is God's story. So many of us have been conditioned to think of our faith as solely an issue of us and God. But faith is a communal experience. A shared journey. I have heard people say their stories are not exciting. I can only imagine how deeply offended God is with comments like this. Not exciting? If the story is about me, then, yes, it is only exciting to a certain degree. But the point of our stories and our faith journeys is that they are about something much bigger. So now that you have heard a bit of Yvette's story, claim it. I tell my story and my wife's story and my friends' stories—I tell every story. I want others to see how they are all connected. So if you think your faith story is boring, take someone else's.

All things are yours.

Being a Christian is not cutting yourself off from real life; it is entering into it more fully.
It is not failing to go deeper; it is going deeper than ever.
It is a journey into the heart of how things really are.

What is it that makes you feel alive? What is it that makes your soul soar?

Recognizing God

A man named Moses is tending his sheep in the land of Midian when he comes upon a burning bush. He moves closer to see more and hears the voice of God, speaking to him about his people and their need to be delivered from the land of Egypt. God tells Moses to take off his sandals, for the ground he is standing on is holy.[20] Moses has been tending sheep in this region for forty years. How many times has he passed by this spot? How many times has he stood in this exact place? And now God tells him the ground is holy?

Has the ground been holy the whole time and Moses is just becoming aware of it for the first time?

Do you and I walk on holy ground all the time, but we are moving so fast and returning so many calls and writing so many emails and having such long lists to get done that we miss it?

Remember Jacob's words after his dream?
"God is in this place, and I wasn't aware of it."

Let's go back to the cliff, planning a wedding with my friends. When they resonate with the peace and harmony of unspoiled nature, I believe God made it unspoiled by speaking it into existence. And Jesus is the life force that makes it possible. So in the deepest sense we can comprehend, my friends are resonating with Jesus, whether they acknowledge it or not. And when they look into each other's eyes and there is love there—real, passionate love, the kind that would lay down its life for another—I believe that love is made possible by God in Jesus. Their laying down their lives is a picture of God doing the same for every single human being in Jesus, whether we affirm it or not. Jesus was up on that cliff with us that day. It is not that God is over here and real life is over there. If it is real, then it's showing us God.

It is not that passion and love and exhilaration are in one place and Jesus is somewhere else.

Wherever you find those, you are finding God.

In affirming and celebrating all that they did that day on the cliff, my friends are closer to Jesus than they could ever imagine.

MOVEMENT FOUR
TASSELS

I could feel my car keys in my pocket, and all I could think about was how far I could be by 11 A.M.

How much gas was in the tank?
How fast could I drive?

Sitting in a chair in a storage room behind the sound booth, I could hear the room filling up with people, and all I wanted to do was leave.

What do you do when you're a pastor of a church, it's Sunday morning, the parking lot is filling with cars, people are finding their seats, the service is about to start, and you are scheduled in a few moments to give the message and you realize you have nothing to say?

How did it come to this? It started out so great . . .

My wife and I and several others started this church called Mars Hill in February of 1999 with dreams of what a revolutionary new kind of community could be.

I was twenty-eight.

What do you know about anything when you're twenty-eight?

But anyway, we did it. We started a church.

People who are starting churches, or want to someday, often ask me when I knew it was time to do it. And I actually have a coherent answer: I knew it was time when I no longer cared if it was "successful."

I'm serious. I had this moment in October 1998 when I realized that if thirteen people joined up with us, and that was all it ever was, that would be okay.

This thing inside of me was so strong that I had to act on it. Can you relate to this feeling? That sense that there is something deep in the fiber of your being that you have to do, and if you don't do it, you will be violating something . . . or somebody?

Better to try and fail, because at least you are being true to yourself.

And the worst thing would be to live wondering, *What if?*

Unleashing a Monster

The dream actually began years before when Kristen and I were living in Los Angeles. We heard about a church called Christian Assembly, so we visited it. What I saw changed everything for me. It was like nothing I had experienced before. This community was exploding with creativity and life—it was like people woke up on Sunday morning and asked themselves, "What would I like to do today more than anything else? How about going to a church service?"

I could not get my mind around this at first.

This concept was so new and fresh—people who gathered because they wanted to.

There wasn't a trace of empty ritual or obligation anywhere in the place. I felt like I was going to see my favorite band. The anticipation. The fact that I would do whatever it took to get there. It didn't matter how far away I had to park. The bond I had with the other people in the room.

Not "I have to" but "I get to."
Not obligation but celebration.
Not duty but desire.

Kristen and I starting attending these services regularly, and then we'd go to the Taco Bell on Colorado Boulevard and talk about what a church could be.

Desire.
Longing.
Come as you are.
Connection.

A group of people who can imagine nothing better than this.

And so several years, two internships, and a cross-country move later, we did it. We started a church in Grand Rapids, Michigan.

Now you have to understand that I started out playing in bands, back when alternative music was . . . alternative. Are there any Pixies fans out there? Talking Heads? Violent Femmes? Midnight Oil? I understood music to be this raw art form that comes from your guts.

Do it yourself.
Strip it down.
Bare bones.
Take away all the fluff and the hype.

This ethos heavily shaped my understandings of what a church should be like: strip everything away and get down to the most basic elements. A group of people desperate to experience God.

Please realize that to this day I have never read a book on church planting or church growth or been to a seminar on how to start a church. I remember being told that a sign had been rented with the church name on it to go in front of the building where we were meeting. I was mortified and had them get rid of it. You can't put a sign out front, I argued; people have to *want* to find us. And so there were no advertisements, no flyers, no promotions, and no signs.

The thought of the word *church* and the word *marketing* in the same sentence makes me sick.

We had these ideas and these dreams, and we went with them.

People would come in, there would be some singing, I would talk about God and Jesus and the Bible and life for about an hour, and then it would be over.

And the strangest thing happened: People came on the first Sunday.

I remember like it was yesterday. A few people came to get me five minutes before the first service and said I had to look out the front windows. I was not prepared for what I saw. Cars and people everywhere. They proceeded to tell me there were traffic jams in every direction; they had run out of chairs; and people were giving up trying to get through the traffic and just pulling over on the side of the road, parking, and walking the rest of the way.

Chaos.
I loved it.

Now I am going to give you some numbers. And I hesitate to do this because few things are more difficult to take than spiritual leaders who are always talking about how big their thing is. But it happened and it's true and it's part of my story.

There were well over 1,000 people there the first Sunday.

People in the aisles. People on the floor. Packed. No more room, not enough chairs.

I ended the message by inviting people to join us on this journey. I talked about the need to explore what a new kind of Christian faith looks like for the new world we find ourselves in. Whatever it was and wherever it led, we were going.

"Join us."
The energy in the place was unreal.

The next morning I held a staff meeting. Which means I sat in my office and thought to myself, *What have I gotten myself into?* Followed closely by, *Sunday's coming again.*

It was during this first week that the practical people stepped forward to be helpful and remind me that people were there out of curiosity the first week and to help me feel encouraged with my new little project. They made sure I understood that I wasn't to get my hopes up, that all these people wouldn't return, and that we'd be able to see in the next few weeks who was really going to be committed to this new church.

You can guess what happened.
More people came the next week.
And even more the following week.

I remember telling people we had no more chairs and if they wanted to bring their friends, they would need to buy chairs for them.

In the next month or two, over two thousand people were showing up on Sundays.

And by September of that first year, we had to hold three services, pushing things to over 4,000 people in the first six months.

A problem developed in the parking lot because people were losing their tempers when they had to wait so long to exit. I heard several stories of harsh words being exchanged and people giving each other the finger. So I stood up one Sunday and said, "If you are here and you aren't a Christian, we are thrilled to have you in our midst. We want you to feel right at home. But if you are here and you're a Christian and you can't even be a Christian in the parking lot, please don't go out into the world and tell people you're a Christian. You'll screw it up for the rest of us. And by the way, we could use your seat."

People cheered.

The more honest, the more raw, the more stripped down we made it, the more people loved it.

We had no five-year plan.
We had no vision statement.
We had no goals.
We had no "demographic."

All we cared about was trying to teach and live the way of Jesus.
It's still all we care about.

So what did I do? I did what anybody else would do in these circumstances: I decided to teach through the book of Leviticus for the first year. Leviticus is one of the first books in the Bible, and it deals with all sorts of ancient ceremonial and sacrificial rites. There are detailed descriptions of what to do with the blood of an animal you have just slaughtered and how to clean yourself after sexual intercourse and how much of your crop needs to be given to the priests. Good stuff.

Around this time we were having problems with too many kids in the classrooms—there wasn't enough oxygen.

And then, several months into it, the fire marshal showed up. Not good. Legal, but not good.

He said we were over code and illegal, and we would have to start turning people away at the doors. We literally had to post people at the doors, and when the room was full, they had to stand there and tell people they weren't legally allowed to go into the service.

I have a friend who couldn't get in the first three times he came.

So we bought a mall. Actually, somebody gave us a mall, and we bought the parking lots surrounding it.

Yes, a mall.

We blew out the walls of the anchor store to make a room big enough to meet in and then turned the other stores into classrooms for kids. A guy came to one of the first services in the mall-turned-church, sat down in a chair, and said, "Hey, I used to shoplift in this exact spot."

So a couple of years into it, Mars Hill is still growing. There were stretches of time when a new staff member was hired every week. House churches were springing up all over the area, partnerships were beginning with other churches around the world, and people who had never been a part of a church were finding a home.

Once again I am going to give you some numbers, and I hesitate to do so, but it is part of the story and it helps to explain the rest. Two years into it, there were around 10,000 people coming to the three gatherings on Sundays.

In the middle of all this growth and chaos was me, superpastor. I was doing weddings and funerals and giving spiritual direction and going to meetings and teaching and dealing with crises and visiting people in prison and at the hospital—the pace and the workload were unreal.

I can't begin to describe what it was like because it was happening so fast. One minute you have these ideas about how it could be and the next minute you are leading this exploding church/event/monster. All of a sudden there are all of these people who know who you are and want something from you and think you're a big deal, and you are the same person you've always been. Everything has changed and yet it hasn't. It's hard to explain, but I found myself asking, "Where is the training manual?"

I think of people who never before cared if I existed who suddenly wanted to be my friends. And that's why I tell you all of this. Because there's a dark side.

It's one thing to be an intern with dreams about how church should be. It's another thing to be the thirty-year-old pastor of a massive church.

And that is why I was sitting there in the closet thinking about how far I could be by 11 A.M. The next service was starting, I had just finished the 9:00 service, and I was done. I escaped to the storage closet where I could be alone and collect myself and figure out what to do next.

I was moments away from leaving the whole thing.
I just couldn't do it anymore.

People were asking me to write articles and books on how to grow a progressive young church, and I wasn't even sure I was a Christian anymore.

I didn't even know if I *wanted* to be a Christian anymore.

What do you do when you can hear the room filling up with thousands of people who are expecting you to give them words from God, and you don't even know if it is true anymore?

I was exhausted.
I was burned out.
I was full of doubt.
I was done.

I had nothing more to say.

And so I sat there with my keys in my hand, turning them over and over, listening to them clink against each other, hearing the room getting louder and louder and more and more full.

And it was at that moment that I made some decisions. Because without pain, we don't change, do we?

I could talk about the dangers of megachurches and life in the spotlight. I could write pages about what is wrong with Church Incorporated and the flaws of institutional Christianity, but I realized that day that things were wrong with the whole way I was living my life.

And if I didn't change, I was not going to make it.

It was in that abyss that I broke and got help . . . because it's only when you hit bottom and are desperate enough that things start to get better. This breakdown, of course, left me with all sorts of difficult decisions to make about Mars Hill. The church was alive and people were being transformed and the stories never stopped coming. Who would leave all that? I decided to be honest about my journey, and if people wanted to come along, great. But I was still going to have to go. And a new journey began, one that has been very, very painful.

And very, very freeing.

It was during this period that I learned that I have a soul.

Shalom

The *tzitzit* (seet-see) first appear in Numbers 15 when God says to Moses, "Throughout the generations to come you are to make tassels on the corners of your garments, with a blue cord on each tassel. You will have these tassels to look at and so you will remember all the commands of the Lord, that you may obey them and not prostitute yourselves by chasing after the lusts of your own hearts and eyes. Then you will remember to obey all my commands."[1]

God tells his people to attach tassels to the corners of their garments so they will be constantly visually reminded to live as he created them to live.

The word in Hebrew here for "corners" is *kanaf.*
The word for "tassel" (or "fringe") is *tzitzit.*

To this day, many Jews wear a prayer shawl to obey this text. The prayer shawl is also in a lot of interesting places throughout the Bible.[2] One of the most significant is in the prophet Malachi's prediction about the coming Messiah: "The sun of righteousness will rise with healing in its wings."[3]

The word Malachi uses for wings is *kanaf*—the same word in Numbers that refers to the edge of a garment, to which the tassels were attached. So a legend grew that when the Messiah came, there would be special healing powers in his *kanaf,* in the tassels of his prayer shawl.

Fast-forward to the time of Jesus: A woman has had an illness for twelve years and no one can cure her.[4] She pushes her way through a crowd to get to Jesus, and when she gets close to him, she grabs his cloak. Now remember, Jesus is a Torah-observant Jewish rabbi who keeps the scripture commandments word for word, including passages like Numbers 15, which means Jesus would have been wearing a prayer shawl. So when the woman grabs the edge of his cloak, she is demonstrating that she believes Jesus is the Messiah and that his tassels have healing powers. She believes that Jesus is who Malachi was talking about.

If you were in the crowd, what would you think about this woman? This woman believes that this man is the Messiah.

She touches his tassels and is healed, just like Malachi said.

But I don't think the physical healing is Jesus's point here. I think it is what Jesus says to her as they part ways.

He says to her, "Go in peace."

The word Jesus would have used for peace is the Hebrew word *shalom*. Shalom is an important word in the Bible, and it is not completely accurate to translate it simply as "peace."

For many of us, we understand peace to be the *absence* of conflict. We talk about peace in the home or in the world or giving peace a chance. But the Hebraic understanding of shalom is far more than just the absence of conflict or strife.

Shalom is the presence of the goodness of God. It's the presence of wholeness, completeness.

So when Jesus tells the woman to go in peace, he is placing the blessing of God on *all* of her. Not just her physical body. He is blessing her with God's presence on her entire being. And this is because for Jesus, salvation is holistic in nature. For Jesus, being saved or reconciled to God involves far more than just the saving of your physical body or your soul—it involves all of you.

God's desire is for us to live in harmony with him—body, soul, spirit, mind, emotions—every inch of our being.

Restoration

To say that salvation is holistic is to acknowledge that there are many dimensions to living in harmony with God. In one sense, salvation is a legal transaction. Humans are guilty because of our sin, and God is the judge who has to deal with our sin because he is holy and any act of sin goes against his core nature. He has to deal with it. Enter Jesus, who dies on the cross in our place. Jesus gets what we deserve; we get what Jesus deserved.

For Jesus, however, salvation is far more. It includes this understanding, but it is far more comprehensive—it is a way of life. To be saved or redeemed or set free is to enter into a totally new way of living in harmony with God. The rabbis called harmony with God *olam haba,* which translates "life in the world to come." Salvation is living more and more in harmony with God, a process that will go on forever.

When we understand salvation from a legal-transaction perspective, then the point of the cross becomes what it has done *for us.* There is the once-and-for-all work of Jesus dying on the cross for our sins and saying, "It is finished." Nothing more to be offered and nothing more to be sacrificed. Jesus's death perfectly satisfies God. We claim this truth as Christians. All has been forgiven. But let's also use a slightly different phrase: the work of the cross *in us.* There is Jesus's death on our behalf once and for all, but there is the ongoing work of the cross in our hearts and minds and souls and lives. There is the ongoing need to return to the cross to be reminded of our brokenness and dependence on God. There is the healing we need from the cross every single day.[5]

Which leads to forgiveness. The point of the cross isn't forgiveness. Forgiveness leads to something much bigger: restoration. God isn't just interested in the covering over of our sins; God wants to make us into the people we were originally created to be. It is not just the removal of what's being held against us; it is God pulling us into the people he originally had in mind when he made us. This restoration is why Jesus always orients his message around becoming the kind of people who are generous and loving and compassionate. The goal here isn't simply to *not* sin. Our purpose is to increase the shalom in this world, which is why approaches to the Christian faith that deal solely with not sinning always fail. They aim at the wrong thing. It is not about what you don't do. The point is becoming more and more the kind of people God had in mind when we were first created.

It is one thing to be forgiven; it is another thing to become more and more and more and more the person God made you to be.

Let me take this further: If we only have a legal-transaction understanding of salvation in which we are forgiven of our sins so we can go to heaven, then salvation essentially becomes a ticket to somewhere else. In this understanding, eternity is something that kicks in when we die. But Jesus did not teach this.

Jesus said that when we believe, we have crossed over from death to life.[6] God always has been and always will be. And when I enter into a relationship with God through Christ, I am connected with God now and I will be connected with God forever. For Jesus, salvation is now.

I need a God for now.
I need healing now.
I need help now.
Yes, even greater things will happen someday.
But salvation is now.

This now leads to another danger of embracing only one dimension of salvation. When faith is defined solely in legal terms, the dominant idea often becomes "inviting

Jesus into your heart," a phrase that is not found anywhere in the Bible. That doesn't mean it is not legitimate;
it just means we have to be careful that we don't adopt
ideas that come with it that aren't what God has in mind.
The problems come when salvation becomes all about
me. Me being saved. Me having my sins forgiven. Me
being reconciled to God.

The Bible paints a much larger picture of salvation. It
describes all of creation being restored. The author of
Ephesians writes that all things will be brought together
under Jesus.[7]

Salvation is the entire universe being brought back into
harmony with its maker.

This has huge implications for how people present the
message of Jesus. Yes, Jesus can come into our hearts.
But we can join a movement that is as wide and deep and
big as the universe itself. Rocks and trees and birds and
swamps and ecosystems. God's desire is to restore all
of it.

The point is not me; it's God.

It is one thing to be saved. To believe in Jesus. It is
another thing to be healed. It is possible to be saved and
miserable. It is possible to be saved and not be a healthy,
whole, life-giving person. It is possible for the cross to
have done something *for* a person but not *in* them.

My Soul

What happened to me is that I realized I believed in Jesus and thought of myself as "saved" and "redeemed" and "reborn," yet massive areas of my life were unaffected. I learned that salvation is for *all* of me. I learned that Jesus wants to heal my soul—now.

And for Jesus to heal my soul, I had to stare my junk right in the face.

There is so much I could say about this healing of the soul, and it has only just begun for me, but a few things have become quite clear.

First, no amount of success can heal a person's soul. In fact, success makes it worse. I speak with great authority on this subject. People were referring to me as the poster boy for the next generation of Christianity. I started a church and a lot of people were coming to hear me speak, and I had things I had never dealt with and they were still there, even after I "made it."

If you have issues surrounding your identity, those issues will not go away if you "make it." They will be there until they are hunted down and identified and dealt with. We often live under the illusion that when we reach that goal and complete our mission, those issues that churn on the inside will go away.

But it's not true.

There is a great saying in the recovery movement: "Wherever you go, there you are."

That's why when we talk with people who are just itching to leave town because they "just need to get out of here," we know they will be back. Often they find out that whatever it is, it went with them. The problem is not the town. The problem is somewhere inside of them.

Success doesn't fix anything. We have the same problems and compulsions and addictions, only now we have *more* stress and *more* problems and *more* pressure.

I used to think—and I'm giving you a window into my insanity here—that when the church got bigger, *then* it would be easier.

Easier?

I don't know if this connects with you, but have you bought into any of these lies? The lies that tell you success and achievement will fix it? They won't. You will be the same person, only you'll have more of everything, and that includes pain.

In addition, there is always a mystery behind the mystery.[8] There is a reason we do what we do, and often it is the result of something that is the result of something that is—you guessed it—the result of something. What happens is we try to fix things, but we stop at the first or second layer. We're stressed and so we make adjustments in time management. But a better question is, why do I take on so much? But an even better question is, why is it so hard for me to say no? Or even, why is that person's approval so important to me?

But that's not even the real issue.

What I have learned is that the deeper you go, the more painful it gets.

We have to be willing to drag up *everything*.

I started going to counseling and discovered that there are things that happened to me when I was thirteen that have shaped me.

Thirteen?

In one moment of enlightenment, my therapist and my wife were helping me drag up specific events from when I was in my early teens. I was remembering them like they were yesterday. I remember the encounter, what was said, what I did, how I reacted, and what it did to me.

Now I come from a family where I was loved and supported, and yet I have junk from way back then. What we discovered is that some of these experiences produced a drive in me to succeed and prove myself and show others . . . sound familiar?

Part of my crash came from my failure to identify these forces until recently. I had been pushing myself and going and going and going and achieving and not even really knowing why.

It is easier to keep going than to stop and begin diving into the root causes.

I think this is why so many pastors have affairs. They don't know how to stop. They are driven and are achieving and are exhausted and don't know how to say they're tired. They are scared to look weak. So they start looking for a way out. They know that a "moral failure" will give them the break they're looking for.

As pastor, I spend a lot of timing dealing with other people's pain. And when I am dealing with theirs, then I don't have to think about my own. I think that's why so many of us push ourselves so hard. As long as I'm going and going and going, I don't have to stop and face my own pain. Stopping is just so difficult.

I learned that most of my life I avoided the abyss because it is the end of the game. There's no more pretending.

It is scary. It is scary to hit the wall because you don't know what it's going to feel like. And you might get hurt.

But what happened to me in that storage room between the 9 and 11 A.M. services, in those agonizing moments of despair, was the best thing that could have happened.

I couldn't go on.
Usually, we can go on. And that's the problem.
We put on the mask, suck it up, and keep going.

We find some extra reserve of strength and pretend like everything's fine, like that incident was just a minor blip that isn't a big deal.

But it is a big deal.

It's a sign that we are barely hanging on. And we ignore these little blips at the risk of our souls. It is only when something deep within us snaps that we are ready to start over and get help.

We have to let the game stop.

I realize this is not groundbreaking news, but when we get desperate and realize we cannot keep living this way, then we have to change. We have no other option, which is why we only change when we hit the abyss. Anything else is like window shopping; we may look for a moment or even try it on, but we aren't taking anything home with us.

As I let all this come spewing forth the first time in my therapist's office, he interrupted me. I was making lists of all the people I was working to keep happy. He said it was clear that there were significant numbers of people I was spending a significant amount of time working to please and that my issue was a simple one.

I was anticipating something quite profound and enlightening as I got out my pen.

He said this: "Sin."

And then he said, in what has become a pivotal moment in my journey, "Your job is the relentless pursuit of who God has made you to be. And anything else you do is sin and you need to repent of it."

The relentless pursuit of who God made me to be.

I started identifying how much of my life was about making sure the right people were pleased with me. And as this became more and more clear, I realized how less and less pleased I was with *myself.* What happens is our lives become so heavily oriented around the expectations of others that we become more and more like them and less and less like ourselves. We become split.

I was split.

I had this person I knew I was made to be, yet it was mixed in with all of these other . . . people. As the lights were turned on, I saw I had all of this guilt and shame because I wasn't measuring up to the image of the perfect person I had in my head. I had this idea of a superpastor—all of these messages I had been sent over the years that I had received and internalized.

Superpastor is always available to everyone and accomplishes great things but always has time to stop and talk and never misses anyone's birthday and if you are sick he's at the hospital and you can call him at home whenever you need advice and he loves meetings and spends hours studying and praying and yet you can interrupt him if you need something—did I mention he always puts his family first?

Now you are starting to see some of my issues.
I am not superpastor.
I don't do well in an office nine to five.
I jump out of my skin if I am in meetings too long.
I am institutionally challenged.

But I am not defined by what I am not. And understanding this truth is a huge part of becoming whole. I had to stop living in reaction and start letting a vision for what lies ahead pull me forward.

I began to sort out with those around me what God did make me to do. What kept coming up was that my life work is fundamentally creative in nature. And creating has its own rhythms, its own pace. Inspiration comes at strange times when you create. And inspiration comes because of discipline. And discipline comes when you organize your life in specific, intentional ways. It means saying yes to certain things and no to other things. And then sticking to it.

I had this false sense of guilt and subsequent shame because I believed deep down that I wasn't working hard enough. And I believed the not-working-hard-enough lie because I didn't function like superpastor, who isn't real anyway.

So I had one choice—I had to kill superpastor.
I had to take him out back and end his pathetic existence.

I went to the leaders of our church and shared with them
my journey as it was unfolding. I told them that if they
needed to release me and find superpastor, I understood.
If we don't know who we are or where we're trying to
go, we put the people around us in an uncomfortable
position. They are doing the best they can with what they
have, but sometimes we haven't given them much, have
we?

And when we begin to pursue becoming the people God
made us to be, we give them more and more to go on.

I meet so many people who have superwhatever rattling
around in their head. They have this person they are
convinced they are supposed to be, and their superwhatever is killing them. They have this image they picked up
over the years of how they are supposed to look and act
and work and play and talk, and it's like a voice that never
stops shouting in their ear.

And the only way to not be killed by it is to shoot first.
Yes, that is what I meant to write.
You have to kill your superwhatever.
And you have to do it right now.

Because your superwhatever will rob you of today and
tomorrow and the next day until you take it out back and
end its life.

Go do it.
The book will be here when you get back.

Healing

There are so many layers to the healing of the soul. One practice that has brought incredible healing is the taking of a Sabbath. Now when we read the word *Sabbath,* most of us think of a day in the week, which is what it is. But I have learned that the real issue behind the Sabbath isn't which day of the week it is but how we live all the time.

I decided to start taking one day a week to cease from work. And what I discovered is that I couldn't even do it at first.

I would go into a depression.
By the afternoon I would be so . . . low.

I realized that my life was all about keeping the adrenaline buzz going and that I was only really happy when I was going all the time. When I stopped to spend a day to remember that I am loved just because I exist, I found out how much of my efforts were about earning something I already have.

Sabbath is taking a day a week to remind myself that I did not make the world and that it will continue to exist without my efforts.

Sabbath is a day when my work is done, even if it isn't.
Sabbath is a day when my job is to enjoy. Period.
Sabbath is a day when I am fully available to myself and those I love most.
Sabbath is a day when I remember that when God made the world, he saw that it was good.
Sabbath is a day when I produce nothing.
Sabbath is a day when I remind myself that I am not a machine.
Sabbath is a day when at the end I say, "I didn't do anything today," and I don't add, "And I feel so guilty."
Sabbath is a day when my phone is turned off, I don't check my email, and you can't get ahold of me.

Jesus wants to heal our souls, wants to give us the shalom of God. And so we have to stop. We have to slow down. We have to sit still and stare out the window and let the engine come to an idle. We have to listen to what our inner voice is saying.[9]

I was with a friend last week who was abused as a young child. She has never dealt with it. She has never faced it and dragged it up and let Jesus heal her. And so we're driving along and she's angry with every other driver and her rage is boiling just below the surface. She has a mystery behind the mystery. Her entire life is affected by what happened to her when she was eight, and she isn't even aware of it. And when it's brought up, she brushes it aside.

Why do we do the things we do? Many people react to and are driven by these deep, unspoken forces. They are strong and they dictate huge areas of our lives. And it is possible to be a good Christian and go to church services and sing the right songs and jump through the right hoops and never let Jesus heal your soul.

Perhaps you have been around Christian communities enough to want nothing to do with them, and one of the reasons is the talk all seems so shallow. Like no one is talking about what really matters. I think this is a direct effect of the state of the souls of many pastors and leaders. So many leaders in Christian communities are going so fast and producing so much and accomplishing so much that they become a shell of a person. There is no space to deal honestly with what's going on deep inside them.

I have seen many leaders who wear their issues on their sleeve. They are raising money to build a bigger building, but the truth is they are still trying to earn their father's approval. They never unplug their answering machine and take a Sabbath because they still believe their parents' divorce was their fault. They live in reaction to everybody around them because no one ever taught them to have a spine. They are racked with guilt because they are not doing enough. They are trying to teach people about a way of life that isn't true of their own life. On a regular basis when I'm with pastors, I'll ask them if the message they are preaching is the dominant reality of their own life. You can't believe how many will say that it isn't.

So my question for leaders—and for Christians everywhere—is, are you smoking what you're selling?

I cannot lead people somewhere I am not trying to go myself. I don't have to have arrived, I don't have to be perfect, but I do need to be on the path. And that's why for so many the church experience has been so shallow— so many leaders have never descended into the depths of their own souls. They haven't done the hard, difficult, gut-wrenching work of shining the bright lights on all of the years of baggage and destructive messages.

It is so hard to look deep inside yourself. My experience has been that very few people do the long, hard work of the soul. Maybe that's why Jesus said the way is narrow.

I'm hoping that wherever you are on your journey, you are tracking with me. I beg you to get help wherever you need it. Go to a counselor. Make an appointment. Go on a retreat. Spend a couple of days in silence. Do whatever it takes.

If you're barely holding on, come clean. Tell somebody. Tell everybody if you have to. Check yourself in some-where. What is it ever going to mean for you to gain the whole world if you lose your soul in the process? (I feel like I've heard that before somewhere.[10])

I say the system has to be changed. It has to be destroyed and replaced not with another system but with an entirely new way of life. I see it happening, and it gives me great hope. I see leaders getting help and refusing to stuff it anymore. I see communities embracing their brokenness and the brokenness of their leaders, and healing is taking place. I see honesty. I see people who want to be fully alive. I see people who want the life Jesus promises and who are willing to let go of ego and prestige and titles to get it.

I can't begin to tell you how much better my life is today than it was several years ago. I continue to dig things up and process new insights and learn about my insides. The journey continues.

I'm learning that a lot of people give up. They settle. And they miss out. Anybody can quit. That's easy.

I'm learning that very few people actually live from their heart. Very few live connected with their soul. And those few who do the difficult work, who stare their junk in the face, who get counsel, who let Jesus into all of the rooms in their soul that no one ever goes in, they make a difference. They are so different; they're coming from such a different place that their voices inevitably get heard above the others. They are pursuing wholeness and shalom, and it's contagious. They inspire me to keep going.

I was sitting in the storage room last week at Mars Hill. The room was filling up for the service at 11 A.M. And I couldn't wait for it to start.

Because Jesus is healing my soul.

MOVEMENT FIVE

DUST

At the center of the Christian faith is this man named Jesus who actually lived. If there wasn't a Bible, there are still lots of historians, some from the first century, who talked about this Jewish man who lived and had followers and died and then, according to his first followers, was alive again.

As his movement gathered steam, this Jewish man came to be talked about more and more as God, fully divine as well as fully human. As his followers talked about him and did what he said and told and retold his stories, the significance of his life began to take on all sorts of cosmic dimensions. They realized that something much bigger was going on here, involving them and the people around them and all of creation. Something involving God making peace with the world and creation being reclaimed and everything in heaven and earth being brought back into harmony with its Creator.

But before all the big language and grand claims, the story of Jesus was about a Jewish man, living in a Jewish region among Jewish people, calling people back to the way of the Jewish God.

When I first began to realize that Jesus was Jewish, I thought, *No way; he was a Christian.*

But as I have learned more about Jesus, the Jewish rabbi, I have come to better understand what it means to follow him. So in this section of the book, I want to take you deep into the first century world of Jesus.

Torah

Jesus grew up in Israel, in an orthodox Jewish region of Israel called Galilee. Now the Jewish people who lived in Galilee believed that at a specific moment in human history, God had spoken directly to their ancestors. They believed this happened soon after their people had been freed from slavery in Egypt and were traveling in the wilderness south of Israel. Their tradition said that while their ancestors were camped at the base of Mount Sinai, their leader, a man named Moses, went up the mountain and received words from God.

They believed not only that God had spoken to Moses but that God had actually given Moses a copy of what he said.

They believed that the first five books of the Bible—
Genesis, Exodus, Leviticus, Numbers, and Deuteronomy—
were a copy of what God had said.

They called these five books the Torah.
Torah can mean teachings or instructions or simply "way."
They believed the Torah was the way, the truth, and the
life.
They believed the best way to live was to live how the
Torah said to live.
And so the central passion of the people of Jesus's world
was teaching, living, and obeying the Torah.

Now the question among the rabbis, the teachers, of
Jesus's day was, how young do you begin teaching the
Bible, the Torah, to kids? One rabbi said, "Under the
age of six we do not receive a child as a pupil; from
six upwards accept him and stuff him [with Torah] like
an ox."[1]

Education wasn't seen as a luxury or even as an option;
education was the key to survival. The Torah was seen as
so central to life that if you lost it, you lost everything. The
first century Jewish historian Josephus said, "Above all
else, we pride ourselves on the education of our children."[2]

So around six years old many Jewish kids would have
gone to school for the first time.[3] It would probably have
been held in the local synagogue and taught by the local
rabbi. This first level of education was called *Bet Sefer*
(which means "House of the Book") and lasted until the
student was about ten years old.

Sometimes the rabbi would take honey and place it on the students' fingers and then have them taste the honey, reminding them that God's words taste like honey on the tongue. The rabbi wanted the students to associate the words of God with the most delicious, exquisite thing they could possibly imagine.

The students would begin memorizing the Torah and by the age of ten would generally know the whole thing by heart.

Genesis.
Exodus.
Leviticus.
Numbers.
Deuteronomy.

Memorized.

Remember, the text was central to life for a Jew living in Galilee in Jesus's day. If you have read the accounts of Jesus's life, have you ever noticed how everybody seems to know the Bible? Jesus quotes a verse, or a phrase from a verse, and everybody seems to know the text. This is because from an early age Jewish people were taking in the words, and they were becoming a part of them.

This memorization was also necessary because if you lived during that time, you didn't have your own copy of the text. The printing press wasn't invented until 1,400 years later. (When you stayed at a hotel in Jesus's day, the Gideons hadn't gotten there first.) Probably your entire village could only afford one copy, which would have been kept in the synagogue in a closet called the Torah ark. There is a good chance you would only *see* the scriptures once a week, and that was when they were brought out of the Torah ark to be read publicly.

Rabbis who taught the Torah were the most respected members of the community. They were the best of the best, the smartest students who knew the text inside and out. Not everybody could be a rabbi.

By age ten, students had begun to sort themselves out. Some would demonstrate natural abilities with the scriptures and distance themselves from the others. These students went on to the next level of education, which was called *Bet Talmud* ("House of Learning") and lasted until sometime around the age of fourteen.

Students who didn't continue their education would continue learning the family trade. If your family made sandals or wine or were farmers, you would apprentice with your parents and extended family as you learned the family trade in anticipation of carrying it on someday and passing it down to the next generation.

Meanwhile, the best of the best, continuing their education in *Bet Talmud,* would then memorize the rest of the Hebrew scriptures. By age thirteen or fourteen the top students had the entire Bible memorized.

Genesis through Malachi . . . thirty-nine books . . . memorized.

A friend of mine studied in the mid-1980s at a yeshiva (Jewish seminary) in Manhattan. He claims he was the only student in the entire school who didn't have the entire Old Testament memorized.

Students in this second step of education would also study the art of questions and the oral tradition surrounding the text. For thousands of years, brilliant minds had been discussing the words of God, wrestling with what they meant and what it meant to live them out. This developed into a massive oral tradition. You had a verse, but then you had all the things that had been said about that verse from all of the different people who had discussed it and wrestled with it and commented on it. A mountain of oral tradition. So as a student, you would be learning the text, but you would also be learning who had said what in the name of whom about it.

Now when the rabbi would ask a student a question, he would seldom give an answer. Have you noticed how rarely Jesus answers questions, but how often he responds with another question?

Rabbis had no interest in having the student spit back information just for information's sake. They wanted to know if the student understood it, if he had wrestled with it. This notion is difficult for the modern mind to grasp because we generally think of education as the transmission of information. The better a student is, the better she is able to produce the right information at the right time.

In the world of rabbinic education, the focus was on questions, which demonstrated that the student not only understood the information but could then take the subject a step further.

By the way, when Jesus's parents found him in the temple area, how old was he? Twelve. Notice what the text says here: "They found him in the temple courts, sitting among the teachers, listening to them and asking them questions. Everyone who heard him was amazed at his understanding and his answers."[4]

Jesus later says to his disciples, "Remember, everything I *learned* I passed on to you."[5]

Did Jesus go to school and learn like the other Jewish kids his age?

Disciples

Around the age of fourteen or fifteen, at the end of *Bet Talmud,* only the best of the best of the best were still studying. Most students by now were learning the family business and starting families of their own.

Those remaining would now apply to a well known rabbi to become one of that rabbi's *talmidim* (disciples). We often think of a disciple as a student, but being a disciple was far more than just being a student. The goal of a disciple wasn't just to know what the rabbi knew, but to *be* just like the rabbi.

This level of education was called *Bet Midrash* ("House of Study"). A student would present himself to a well known rabbi and say, "Rabbi, I want to become one of your disciples."

When a student applied to a rabbi to be one his *talmidim,* he was desiring to take that rabbi's yoke upon him. He wanted to learn to do what the rabbi did.

So when this student came to the rabbi and said, "I want to follow you," the rabbi wanted to know a few things: Can this student do what I do? Can this kid spread my yoke? Can this kid be like me? Does this kid have what it takes?

The rabbi would then question the student. Questions about Torah, about tradition, about other rabbis. Questions about the prophets and the sages and the oral law. Questions about interpretation and legislation. Questions about words and phrases and passages.

The rabbi would grill this teenage kid because he wanted to know if this kid could do what he did. The rabbi did not have time to train a kid who wouldn't ultimately be able to do what he did.

If the rabbi decided that this kid did not have what it took, if this student was not the best of the best, then he would send the student home. He might say, "You obviously love God and know the Torah, but you do not have what it takes to be one of my *talmidim*." And then he might add, "Go home and continue learning the family business."

But if the rabbi believed that this kid did have what it took, he would say, "Come, follow me."

The student would probably leave his father and mother, leave his synagogue, leave his village and his friends, and devote his life to learning how to do what his rabbi did.[6]

He would follow the rabbi everywhere. He would learn to apply the oral and written law to situations. He gave up his whole life to be just like his rabbi.

A friend of mine was in Israel a few years ago and saw a rabbi go into a bathroom and his *talmidim* followed him. They didn't want to miss anything the rabbi might say or do.

This kind of devotion is what it means to be a disciple.

One of the earliest sages of the Mishnah, Yose ben Yoezer, said to disciples, "Cover yourself with the dust of [your rabbi's] feet."

This idea of being covered in the dust of your rabbi came from something everybody had seen. A rabbi would come to town, and right behind him would be this group of students, doing their best to keep up with the rabbi as he went about teaching his yoke from one place to another. By the end of a day of walking in the dirt directly behind their rabbi, the students would have the dust from his feet all over them.

And that was a good thing.

So at the age of thirty, when a rabbi generally began his public teaching and training of disciples, we find Jesus walking along the Sea of Galilee.[7]

"He saw two brothers, Simon called Peter and his brother Andrew. They were casting a net into the lake, for they were fishermen."

Why are they fishermen?

Because they aren't disciples. They weren't good enough; they didn't make the cut.

Jesus calls the not-good-enoughs.

The story continues: "At once they left their nets and followed him."

This is strange, isn't it? Why do they just drop their nets? Why would they quit their jobs for some rabbi they had never met? And those Christian movies don't help. Jesus is usually wearing a white bathrobe with a light blue beauty pageant sash, and his hair is blow-dried and his eyes are glazed over . . .

and he's Swedish.

But given the first century context, it's clear what is going on here. Can you imagine what this must have been like—to have a rabbi say, "Come, follow me"?

To have a rabbi say, "*You* can be like *me*"?

Of course you would drop your net. The rabbi believes you can do what he does. He thinks you can be like him.

Jesus then comes upon James and John, who are fishing with their father, Zebedee. They are apprentices, learning the family business, which in this case happens to be fishing.

If they are still with their father, then how old are they? Fourteen, fifteen, sixteen? Twenty?

Jesus took some boys who didn't make the cut and changed the course of human history.

Now being a disciple was terrifying and exhilarating and demanding—they never knew what the rabbi would do next. One account in the book of Matthew says that Jesus was talking to his disciples at Caesarea Philippi. This is one of those details that is easy to skip, but it is significant. Caesarea Philippi was the world center of the goat god, Pan. People came from all over the world to worship this god. There is a cliff with a giant crack in it that the followers of Pan believed was the place where the spirits from hell would come and go from the earth. The crack was called the Gates of Hell. They built a temple for Pan there and then a court next to it where people would engage in sexual acts with goats during the Pan worship festivals.[8]

And Jesus is there with his disciples. As good Jewish boys, they never would have gone to this place before. It is twenty-six miles from Galilee, where Jesus and his disciples are from. What was that walk like? Did Jesus even tell his disciples where they were going? Can you imagine them talking to each other behind his back? "When our parents find out about this, we are so busted!" The whole experience would have been riveting. Where are we going? What are we doing? What is our rabbi going to do next?

He tells them at Caesarea Philippi that upon this rock he is going to build his new witnessing community, and the Gates of Hell won't be able to stop it. He is essentially saying that those kinds of people—the ones with the goats—are going to join the Jesus movement and it will be unstoppable. How would you as a disciple even begin to process this statement?

Rabbis were passionate and funny and quirky and unpredictable. They told stories and laughed and went to a lot of parties and never stopped asking questions and pushing their students and keeping them guessing. Rabbis devoted their energies to their students to help them learn to do what they did, and they used every opportunity they had to prepare their students.

"I Chose You"

At one point, Jesus's disciples are riding in a boat and Jesus comes walking by on the water. And one of the disciples says, "If it's you, let me come to you on the water."

It's a weird story, isn't it?

And it gets even weirder when the disciple Peter jumps out of the boat because he wants to walk on water like Jesus.

But it makes sense—maybe not the water part, but the disciple part.

If you are a disciple, you have committed your entire life to being like your rabbi. If you see your rabbi walk on water, what do you immediately want to do? Walk on water.

So this disciple gets out on the water and he starts to sink, so he yells, "Jesus save me!"

And Jesus says, "You of little faith, why did you doubt?"
Who does Peter lose faith in?
Not Jesus; Jesus is doing fine.
Peter loses faith in himself.
Peter loses faith that he can do what his rabbi is doing.

If the rabbi calls you to be his disciple, then he believes you can actually be like him. As we read the stories of Jesus's life with his *talmidim,* his disciples, what do we find frustrates him to no end? When his disciples lose faith in themselves.

He even says to them at one point, "You did not choose me, but I chose you."[9]

The entire rabbinical system was based on the rabbi having faith in his disciples.

Let's spend some time here, because the implications of this truth are astounding. A rabbi would only pick a disciple who he thought could actually do what he was doing. Notice how many places in the accounts of Jesus's life he gets frustrated with his disciples.[10] Because they are incapable? No, because of how capable they are. He sees what they could be and could do, and when they fall short, it provokes him to no end. It isn't their failure that's the problem; it's their greatness. They don't realize what they are capable of.

So at the end of his time with his disciples, Jesus has some final words for them. He tells them to go to the ends of the earth and make more disciples.[11] And then he leaves. He promises to send his Spirit to guide them and give them power, but Jesus himself leaves the future of the movement in their hands. And he doesn't stick around to make sure they don't screw it up. He's gone. He trusts that they can actually do it.

God has an incredibly high view of people. God believes that people are capable of amazing things.

I have been told that I need to believe in Jesus. Which is a good thing. But what I am learning is that Jesus believes in me.

I have been told that I need to have faith in God. Which is a good thing. But what I am learning is that God has faith in me.

The rabbi thinks we can be like him.

NEW

I was having lunch with a guy who was telling me about a struggle he had been having for a while. He said he knew he was a sinner and that he was fallen and that he would keep committing this one sin, and he knew he was going to keep committing this one sin because he was a sinner and his nature was evil and there was nothing he could do about it because of what a sinner he was . . .

Do I have to go on?

I was so depressed I wanted to bang my head on the table. His question was basically, why do I struggle like this?

And all that was running through my head during his questions was that his system was perfectly designed to achieve the results he was getting.

He's convinced he is a sinner, he's convinced he is going to sin, he has no hope against sin, he believes his basic nature is sin, and then he wonders why he keeps sinning.

And what was so startling to me is that he said he had just become a Christian.

It seemed to me that becoming a Christian had given him all sorts of new things to feel guilty about. I wondered if becoming a Christian had made his life not better but actually worse.

And then a little while later I had a similar experience. I was listening to a pastor speak, and his point was that people weren't reading their Bibles enough and weren't praying enough and weren't being spiritual enough. If people would just do more—read their Bibles more and pray more and be more spiritual—basically just more "mores," then God would be happy with them.

I felt terrible. What was the point of even trying?

It's not that praying and reading the Bible are bad; it's just that I wanted to do them less and less the more and more he talked.

It wasn't so much what he was saying as it was the place he was coming from. The beginning premise seemed that we are bad and don't do enough, and if we are made to feel guilty enough about it, then we will change our behavior.

I don't think this is what Jesus had in mind.

His greatest anger was reserved for religious leaders who weighed people down with guilt and shame. He says to a group of Bible scholars and teachers, "You experts in the law, woe to you, because you load people down with burdens they can hardly carry, and you yourselves will not lift one finger to help them."[1]

A little while later he calls them "sons of hell."

He goes on to say that it is possible for religious leaders to actually get in the way of people entering into the life of God.[2]

So what is the message? How should people feel about themselves?

Have you ever heard a Christian say, "I'm just a sinner"? I can't find one place in the teachings of Jesus, or the Bible for that matter, where we are to identity ourselves first and foremost as sinners. Now this doesn't mean that we don't sin; that's obvious. In the book of James it's written like this: "We all stumble in many ways."[3] Once again, the greatest truth of the story of Adam and Eve isn't that it happened, but that it *happens.* We all make choices to live outside of how God created us to live. We have all come up short.[4]

Who We Are Now

The first Christians insisted that when we become Christians, a profound change occurs in our fundamental identity. In who we are at the core of our being. In who we are first and foremost, before we are anything else. In our awareness of ourselves. The first Christians were convinced that in identifying with Jesus's death on the cross, something within us dies. They called this person who died the "old man" or the "old woman." The person we were before we had a spiritual birth.[5]

Now this idea of death and rebirth is not a new idea—it has been around in almost every religious tradition since people first started talking about these things. But the first Christians believed that this idea had been lived out in a new and unique way in Jesus's death and resurrection. Paul put it like this in the book of Colossians: "For you died, and your life is now hidden with Christ in God."[6]

So this old nature of mine—the one that was constantly pulling me down and causing me to live in ways I wasn't created to live—has died. And no matter how many times that old nature raises its ugly head and pretends to be alive, it is dead.

And not only did that old person die, but I have been given a new nature.

Again, Paul writes in Colossians, "You have been raised with Christ."[7] I have this new life, this new identity that has been given to me. I have taken on the identity of Christ.

Paul continues, "You used to walk in these ways, in the life you once lived." These first Christians kept insisting that something so transformational was happening in the lives of followers of Jesus that they could refer to their old lives as "the life [we] once lived."[8]

It is not that we are perfect now or that we will never have to struggle. Or that the old person won't come back from time to time. It's that this new way of life involves a constant, conscious decision to keeping dying to the old so that we can live in the new. Paul describes it as Christ *being* our lives.

Paul goes so far as to insist in another letter that if we are having this new kind of transforming experience with Christ in which we are taking on a new identity, we are literally now a "new creation."[9]

I am being remade.
I am not who I was.
I am a new creation.
I am "in Christ."
When God looks at me, God sees Christ, because I'm "in" him.
God's view of me is Christ.
And Christ is perfect.[10]

This is why Paul goes on to say, "Therefore, as God's chosen people, holy and dearly loved . . . "[11]

Did you catch that word in the middle?
Holy.

Not "going to be holy someday." Not "wouldn't it be nice if you were holy, but instead you're a mess." But "holy."

Holy means pure, without blemish, unstained.
In these passages we're being told *who we are,* now.

The issue then isn't my beating myself up over all of the things I am not doing or the things I am doing poorly; the issue is my learning who this person is who God keeps insisting I *already am.*

Notice these words from the letter to the Philippians: "Let us live up to what we have already attained."[12]

There is this person who we already are in God's eyes.
And we are learning to live like it is true.

This is an issue of identity. It is letting what God says about us shape what we believe about ourselves. This is why shame has no place whatsoever in the Christian experience. It is simply against all that Jesus is for. As the writer to the Romans put it, "Therefore, there is now no condemnation for those who are in Christ Jesus."[13]

None.
No shame.
No list of what is being held against us.
No record of wrongs.
It has simply been done away with.

It is no longer an issue.
Bringing it up is pointless.
Beating myself up is pointless.

Beating others up about who and what they are not is going the wrong direction. It is working against the purposes of God. God is not interested in shaming people; God wants people to see who they really are.

"Let us live up to what we have already attained."
I am not who I was.
You are not who you were.
Old person going away, new person here, now.
Reborn, rebirthed, remade, reconciled, renewed.

Jesus put it this way: "You are in me and I am in you."[14]

So when the first Christians went all over the Roman Empire telling people the Jesus message, they spent most of their time explaining who people are from God's perspective. Who we already are. They insisted that people can live a new life, counting ourselves "dead to sin but alive to God."[15]

When we stumble and fall back into old patterns, we call them what they are: old patterns. Old ways. Old habits of the old person.

Something new is happening inside us.

Jesus said that as this new reality takes over our hearts and lives and minds and actions, we are crossing over "from death to life."[16] He called this new kind of life "eternal life." For Jesus, eternal life wasn't a state of being for the future that we would enter into somewhere else; it is a quality of life that starts now.

Eternal life then is a certain kind of life I am living more and more now and will go on forever.[17] I am living more and more in connection with God, and I will live connected with God forever.

This has huge implications for when I do stumble, when I sin and the old person comes back from the dead for a few moments.

I admit it.
I confess it.
I thank God I am forgiven.
I make amends with anyone who has been affected by my actions.
And then I move on.

Not because sin isn't serious, but because I am taking seriously who God says I am. The point isn't my failure; it is God's success in remaking me into the person he originally intended me to be.

God's strength, not mine.
God's power, not mine.

So what does this mean for the Christian life? To begin, Christians are people learning who they are in Christ. We are being taught about our new identity. Do you see how deeply this new identity affects the life of a community? I heard a teacher say that if people were taught more about who they are, they wouldn't have to be told what to do.[18] It would come naturally. When we see religious communities spending most of their time trying to convince people not to sin, we are seeing a community that has missed the point. The point isn't sin management.[19] The point is who we are now.

Often communities of believers in the New Testament are identified as "saints." The word *saints* is a translation of the Greek word *hagios,* which means "holy or set apart ones." Those who are "in Christ." Not because of what they have done, but because of what God has done. There is nothing we can do, and there is nothing we ever could have done, to earn God's favor. We already have it.

Jesus tells a parable about a young son who leaves home, hits bottom, and returns in shame. His father sees him from far off, runs to him, embraces him, and announces a party in honor of his homecoming.

In this story, God is the God who stands in the driveway, waiting for his kids to come home.

So the party starts and everybody is celebrating, and the older brother comes in from the field mad. He wants to know why his brother gets a party and he doesn't. The parable ends with the father telling the older son, "You are always with me, and everything I have is yours." The father wants the older son to know that everything he wants he has always had; there is nothing he could ever do to earn it. The elder son's problem isn't that he doesn't have anything; it's that he has had it all along but refused to trust that it was really true.[20]

We cannot earn what we have always had. What we can do is trust that what God keeps insisting is true about us is actually true.

Let's take this further. As one writer puts it, "While we were still sinners, Christ died for us."[21] While we were unable to do anything about our condition, while we were helpless, while we were unaware of just how bad the situation was, Jesus died.

And when Jesus died on the cross, he died for everybody.
Everybody.
Everywhere.
Every tribe, every nation, every tongue, every people group.[22]

Jesus said that when he was lifted up, he would draw all people to himself.[23]
All people. Everywhere.
Everybody's sins on the cross with Jesus.

So this reality, this forgiveness, this reconciliation, is true for everybody. Paul insisted that when Jesus died on the cross, he was reconciling "all things, in heaven and on earth, to God."[24] All things, everywhere.

This reality then isn't something we make true about ourselves by doing something. It is already true. Our choice is to live in this new reality or cling to a reality of our own making.

God is retelling each of our stories in Jesus. All of the bad parts and the ugly parts and the parts we want to pretend never happened are redeemed. They seemed pointless and they were painful at the time, but God retells our story and they become the moments when God's grace is most on display. We find ourselves asking, am I really forgiven of *that*? The fact that we are loved and accepted and forgiven in spite of everything we have done is simply too good to be true. Our choice becomes this: We can trust his retelling of the story, or we can trust our telling of our story. It is a choice we make every day about the reality we are going to live in.

And this reality extends beyond this life.
Heaven is full of forgiven people.
Hell is full of forgiven people.
Heaven is full of people God loves, whom Jesus died for.
Hell is full of forgiven people God loves, whom Jesus died for.

The difference is how we choose to live, which story we choose to live in, which version of reality we trust.

Ours or God's.

When we choose God's vision of who we are, we are living as God made us to live. We are living in the flow of how we are going to live forever. This is the life of heaven, here and now. And as we live this life, in harmony with

God's intentions for us, the life of heaven becomes more and more present in our lives. Heaven comes to earth. This is why Jesus taught his disciples to pray, "May your will be done on earth as it is in heaven." There is this place, this realm, heaven, where things are as God desires them to be. As we live this way, heaven comes here. To this place, this world, the one we're living in.

Two Realms

Now if there is a life of heaven, and we can choose it, then there's also another way. A way of living out of sync with how God created us to live. The word for this is *hell:* a way, a place, a realm absent of how God desires things to be. We can bring heaven to earth; we can bring hell to earth.

For Jesus, heaven and hell were present realities. Ways of living we can enter into here and now. He talked very little of the life beyond this one because he understood that the life beyond this one is a continuation of the kinds of choices we make here and now.

For Jesus, the question wasn't, "How do I get into heaven?" but "How do I bring heaven here?"

The question wasn't, "How do I get *in there?*" but "How do I get there *here?*"

I was in Rwanda two years ago doing research on the AIDS crisis. It had been almost ten years since the massacre of 1994 when over 800,000 Rwandans were killed by their fellow countrymen. Yet driving down the street, we passed person after person missing an arm or a leg. Children who had been struck with a sword were now high school students walking along with a crutch or sitting in a wheelchair.

If you do any reading on what happened in Rwanda, the word that you'll read most often used to describe it is *hell.*

A hell on earth.

When people use the word *hell,* what do they mean? They mean a place, an event, a situation absent of how God desires things to be. Famine, debt, oppression, loneliness, despair, death, slaughter—they are all hell on earth.

Jesus's desire for his followers is that they live in such a way that they bring heaven to earth.

What's disturbing then is when people talk more about hell after this life than they do about hell here and now. As a Christian, I want to do what I can to resist hell coming to earth. Poverty, injustice, suffering—they are all hells on earth, and as Christians we oppose them with all our energies. Jesus told us to.

Jesus tells a parable about the kind of people who will live with God forever. It is a story of judgment, of God evaluating the kind of lives people have lived. First he deals with the "righteous," who gave food to the hungry, gave water to the thirsty, welcomed the stranger, clothed the naked, and visited the prisoner. These are the kind of people who spend forever with God. Jesus measures their eternal standings in terms of not what they said or believed but how they lived, specifically in regard to the hell around them.

The judge then condemns a group of people because they didn't take care of the needy and naked and hurting in their midst. They chose hell instead of heaven, and God gives them what they wanted.[25]

For Jesus, this new kind of life in him is not about escaping this world but about making it a better place, here and now. The goal for Jesus isn't to get into heaven. The goal is to get heaven here.

Jesus tells another story about a rich man and a beggar who lies outside the rich man's gates. The rich man dies and goes to hell, while the beggar dies and goes to "Abraham's side," a Jewish way of describing heaven. This is the one story Jesus tells in which somebody is actually in hell after they have died. What is the reason? According to the details of the story, the rich man refused to be generous with the poor man, letting him live a hell on earth right outside his front door.

On another occasion, Jesus is asked to mediate in a monetary dispute between two brothers. Jesus uses the moment to tell a story about a man whose crops do well and who becomes rich. He then decides not to share the bounty but to build bigger barns for storage and then take it easy for the rest of his days. Jesus told this story at a time when many of his countrymen were losing family land and having trouble feeding their families. Being hungry was a very real issue for a lot of people. In the story, God is so offended by the man's selfish actions that his very life is taken from him that night. It is one of the only places in all of Jesus's teachings where someone does something so horrible in Jesus's eyes that they deserve to die right away. And what is this horrible thing the man did? He refused to be generous. He brought hell to earth.

Jesus wants his followers to bring heaven, not hell, to earth. This has been God's intention for people since the beginning. Jesus is not teaching anything new for his day. God walked in the garden, looking for Adam and Eve.[26] God told the Israelites to build a tabernacle so he could live in their midst.[27] King Solomon built a temple, God's house, so God could live permanently among his people. And when Jesus comes, he's referred to as God "taking on flesh and dwelling among us." Another translation of this verse is, "The word became flesh and blood and moved into the neighborhood."[28]

The entire movement of the Bible is of a God who wants to be here, with his people. The church is described later as being the temple of God.[29] And how does the Bible end? With God "coming down" and taking up residence here on earth.[30]

True spirituality then is not about escaping this world to some other place where we will be forever. A Christian is not someone who expects to spend forever in heaven there. A Christian is someone who anticipates spending forever here, in a new heaven that comes to earth.

The goal isn't escaping this world but making this world the kind of place God can come to. And God is remaking us into the kind of people who can do this kind of work.

T'shuva

The remaking of this world is why Jesus's first messages began with "*T'shuva,* for the kingdom of heaven has come near."[31]

The Hebrew word *t'shuva* means "to return." Return to the people we were originally created to be. The people God is remaking us into.

God makes us in his image. We reflect the beauty and creativity and wonder of the God who made us. And Jesus calls us to return to our true selves. The pure, whole people God originally intended us to be, before we veered off course.

Somewhere in you is the you whom you were made to be.

We need you to be you.
We don't need a second anybody. We need the first you.

The problem is that the image of God is deeply scarred in each of us, and we lose trust in God's version of our story. It seems too good to be true. And so we go searching for identity. We achieve and we push and we perform and we shop and we work out and we accomplish great things, longing to repair the image. Longing to find an identity that feels right.

Longing to be comfortable in our own skin.

But the thing we are searching for is not somewhere else. It is right here. And we can only find it when we give up the search, when we surrender, when we trust. Trust that God is already putting us back together.

Trust that through dying to the old, the new can give birth. Trust that Jesus can repair the scarred and broken image.

It is trusting that I am loved. That I always have been. That I always will be. I don't have to do anything. I don't have to prove anything or achieve anything or accomplish one more thing. That exactly as I am, I am totally accepted, forgiven, and there is nothing I could ever do to lose this acceptance.[32]

God knew exactly what he was doing when he made you. There are no accidents. We need you to embrace your true identity, who you are in Christ, letting this new awareness transform your life.

That is what Jesus has in mind.
That is what brings heaven to earth.

I was having breakfast with my dad and my younger son at the Real Food Café on Eastern Avenue just south of Alger in Grand Rapids. We were finishing our meal when I noticed that the waitress brought our check and then took it away and then brought it back again. She placed it on the table, smiled, and said, "Somebody in the restaurant paid for your meal. You're all set." And then she walked away.

I had the strangest feeling sitting there. The feeling was helplessness. There was nothing I could do. It had been taken care of. To insist on paying would have been pointless. All I could do was trust that what she said was true was actually true and then live in that. Which meant getting up and leaving the restaurant. My acceptance of what she said gave me a choice: to live like it was true or to create my own reality in which the bill was not paid.

This is our invitation. To trust that we don't owe anything. To trust that something is already true about us, something has already been done, something has been there all along.

To trust that grace pays the bill.

GOOD

It is such a letdown to rise from the dead and have your friends not recognize you.

The writer John tells us that Mary saw Jesus after his resurrection but did not realize it was Jesus. Jesus asked her, "Woman, why are you crying? Who is it you are looking for?"

"Thinking he was the gardener, she said . . ."[1]

I love that line "thinking he was the gardener." It is so loaded. Jewish writers like John did things like this all the time in their writings. They record what seem to be random details, yet in these details we find all sorts of multiple layers of meaning.[2] There are even methods to help decipher all the hidden meanings in a text. One is called the principle of first mention. Whenever you come across a significant word in a passage, find out where this word first appears in the Bible. John does this in his gospel. The first mention of the word *love* is in 3:16—"For

God so loved the world that he gave his one and only Son." We then discover that *love* is first mentioned in Genesis 22 when God tells Abraham to take "your son, your only son, Isaac, whom you love" and offer him as a sacrifice. John is doing something intentional in his gospel: He wants his readers to see a connection between Abraham and his son, and God and God's son. John's readers who knew the Torah would have seen the parallels right away.

Back to the empty tomb and Mary's inability to recognize Jesus. She mistakes him for a gardener. Where is the first mention of a garden in the Bible? Genesis 2, the story of God placing the first people in a . . . garden. And what happens to this garden and these people? They choose to live outside of how God made them to live, and they lose their place in the garden. Death enters the picture and paradise is lost.

John tells us that Jesus is buried in a garden tomb. And Jesus is mistaken for a gardener. Something else is going on here. John wants us to see a connection between the garden of Eden and Jesus rising from the dead in a garden. There is a new Adam on the scene, and he is reversing the curse of death by conquering it.[3] As one writer put it, "It was impossible for death to keep its hold on him."[4] And he's doing it in a garden. He's reclaiming creation. He's entering into it and restoring it and renewing God's plans for the world.

Jesus is God's way of refusing to give up on his dream for the world.

Our Environment

To look at God's restoration plans in greater depth, we need to go back to how God creates the world and what he thinks about it. The Bible starts with God making the ground and the seas and calling them "good." God makes land that produces vegetation and it is "good." Over and over this word *good* is used to describe how God perceives what he has made. It is all "good."

Notice what God does with his "good" creation. "Then God said, 'Let the *land* produce vegetation: seed-bearing plants and trees on the land that bear fruit with seed in it, according to their various kinds.' And it was so." The next verse is significant: "The *land* produced vegetation."[5] Notice that it doesn't say, "God produced vegetation." God empowers the land to do something. He gives it the capacity to produce trees and shrubs and plants and bushes that produce fruit and seeds. God empowers creation to make more.

This happens again in Genesis 1:22 when God blesses the creatures of the water and sky and then says, "Be fruitful and increase in number and fill the water in the seas, and let the birds increase on the earth." Once again God gives creation—here it is fish and birds—the ability to multiply and make more. God doesn't make more fish; God gives fish the ability to make more.

An important distinction.

God empowers creation to make more and in doing so loads it with potential. It is going to grow and change and move and not be the same today as it was yesterday, and tomorrow it will move another day forward. Creation is loaded with potential and possibility and promise.

God then makes people whom he puts right in the middle of all this loaded creation, commanding them to care for creation, to manage it, to lovingly use it, to creatively order it. The words he gives are words of loving service and thoughtful use. From day one (which is really day six), they are in intimate relationship and interaction with their environment. They are environmentalists. Being deeply connected with their environment is who they are. For them to be anything else or to deny their divine responsibility to care for all that God has made would be to deny something that is at the core of their existence.

This is why litter and pollution are spiritual issues.

And until that last sentence makes perfect sense, we haven't fully grasped what it means to be human and live in God's world. Everyone is an environmentalist. We cannot live independently of the world God has placed us in. We are intimately connected. By God.

Not only are we connected with creation, but creation is going to move forward. It can't help it. It is loaded with energy. It's going to grow and produce and change and morph. This point is central to the story: The garden of Eden is not perfect.[6] Nowhere in Genesis does it say it is perfect. The word the Bible uses is *good*. There is a difference. When we say "perfect," what we generally mean is "static" or "fixed" or "unchanging." It has reached a state in which there is going to be no more change. But this is not what Genesis says about the garden of Eden. Good means changing and growing and advancing and producing *new* things. And so these people are placed in the midst of this dynamic, changing, alive, vibrant environment and charged with the divine responsibility of doing something with it. Creating, arranging, ordering, caring for—doing something with it.

These first people have a choice: to do something with it in harmony with God or to use it for their own purposes. And not doing something with it is a choice as well. It would be a sin to abuse creation and distort it and rape it and exploit it, but it would also be a sin to do nothing with it. Because doing nothing with it would essentially be saying to God, "You have made nothing of interest to me."[7]

So the issue of eating the fruit then is far bigger than Adam and Eve simply disobeying God. They are throwing off the whole deal. God made this magnificent world with endless possibilities of creativity and beauty and meaning, and they miss it. They decide to steer the thing in a different direction. A direction of their choosing.

God has given us power and potential and ability. God has given this power to us so we will *use it well.* We have choices about how we are going to use our power. The choices of the first people were so toxic because they were placed in the middle of a complex web of

interaction and relationships with the world God had
made. When they sinned, their actions threw off the
balance of everything.

Weather.
Trees.
Oceans.

It is all one, and when one part starts to splinter and
fracture, the whole thing starts to crumble. These people
cannot be separated from their environment. One part
falls out of harmony, and everything is affected. As one
text says, "The whole creation has been groaning."[8] It is
all thrown off.

This is how the Bible starts.
Unlimited potential.
Unbelievable promise and possibility.
And then fracturing, splintering, chaos.

Moving Forward

Will creation always be like this? Fractured? Chaotic? This
has been the question for thousands of years. And central
to the Jewish world of Jesus was the belief that God not
only hadn't given up on creation but was also actively
at work within it, bringing it back to how he originally
intended it to be. The prophets had a way of talking
about this restoration movement of God's. They spoke of
God reclaiming the earth and restoring the world. They
did not talk about people going somewhere else at the

end of time. They talked about God coming here at the end of time.[9]

Notice what Jesus says about the end of the world in Matthew: "Truly I tell you, at the renewal of all things, when the Son of Man sits on his glorious throne . . ."[10]

Jesus uses an important word here: *renewal.*
Jesus describes his return as a rebirth, a regeneration, a renewal.

Remember, when God made the world, he called it good. Why would God destroy something he thinks is good?

Notice what Peter says in the book of Acts about the same event: "Heaven must receive [Jesus] until the time comes for God to restore everything, as he promised long ago through his holy prophets."[11] Big word Peter uses here: *restore.* To restore is to make things how they once were. To renovate, to rebuild, to put back together the parts that are broken.

As Paul put it in Colossians, "For God was pleased to have all his fullness dwell in [Jesus], and through him to reconcile to himself all things, whether things on earth or things in heaven, by making peace through his blood, shed on the cross."[12] Paul uses another significant word here: *reconcile.* To make peace where it has been lacking. To bring back together. To mend what is torn and to fix what is broken. And Paul wants us to make sure we grasp that this is a much larger issue than just human souls. He uses the phrase "all things, whether things on earth or things in heaven" because he wants us to see that this is all of creation. "All things" really means "everything"— every bird and tree and mountain and star and every single square inch of the physical creation.

In Jesus, God is putting it all back together.

To make the cross of Jesus just about human salvation is to miss that God is interested in the saving of everything. Every star and rock and bird. All things.

And God isn't just interested in reclaiming his original dream for creation; he wants to take it further. Imagine if you took all the sin and death out of the Bible. You would be left with a short book. It would have four chapters to be exact: Genesis 1 and 2; Revelation 21 and 22. In Genesis 1 and 2, we are told of a garden, but in Revelation 21 and 22, we are told of a city. A city is more advanced, more complicated than a garden. If a garden is developed and managed and cared for, it is eventually going to turn into a city. If there was no sin or death, creation would still move forward because God doesn't just want to reclaim things; God wants to see them move forward.

A New Culture

Let's return to the garden, to Jesus rising from the dead, having conquered death. The early community of Jesus's followers saw in his resurrection the moment their people had been waiting for: God continuing, but in a new and significant way, the restoration of the world. Paul goes so far as to say that Jesus's resurrection was the firstfruits—a very Jewish way of saying, "Hang on, there's more to come."[13]

In the first century, this claim of restoration had numerous social, political, and economic dimensions to it. The world was ruled by the Roman Empire, and the Roman Empire was ruled by a succession of emperors called the caesars. The caesars claimed they were sent by the gods to renew creation. Caesar Augustus believed that as the son of god, he was god incarnate on earth, the prince of peace who had come to restore all of creation. He inaugurated a twelve-day celebration called Advent to celebrate his birth. Sound familiar? His priests offered sacrifices and incense to rid people of their guilt. One of his popular slogans was "There is no other name under heaven by which men can be saved than that of Caesar." Another phrase they used often was "Caesar is Lord." Throughout the Roman Empire, the caesars called on people to worship them as the divine saviors of humankind, and a city that acknowledged Caesar as Lord was called an *ekklesia.*[14]

Being a citizen of the Roman Empire was significant. It was membership in the most powerful kingdom ever. All of society, for that matter, was ranked and ordered. Roman citizens were higher status than non-Roman citizens. Men were ranked higher than women. Slave owners and those who were free were ranked above slaves, who were seen as property to be owned. And then there were the masses—the majority of the population who weren't the elite, ruling class. Everybody had their place in society.

It was at this time, in this world, that the Jesus movement exploded among an ethnic minority in a remote corner of the empire. These people claimed their leader was a rabbi who had announced the arrival of the kingdom of God, had been crucified, and had risen from the dead and appeared to his followers. One of their favorite slogans was "Jesus is Lord."[15]

Take a minute to reflect on the political dimensions of that claim. If Jesus is Lord, then what does that say about Caesar? These first Christians were subverting the entire order of the empire, claiming that there was a Lord, and he wasn't Caesar. And what did they call their gatherings? *Ekklesias.*[16] A word that translates in English as "church." Another of their favorite slogans was "There is no other name given under heaven by which we must be saved than that of Jesus."[17] Shocking. They took political propaganda from the empire and changed the words to make it about their Lord. To join up with these people was to risk your life. And not only this, but they made claims about the whole way society was structured.

In a letter to a church in a region called Galatia, one of the first Christians, Paul, claimed that "in Christ"—the phrase Christians used to describe this new reality—there was "neither Jew nor Gentile, neither slave nor free, neither male nor female."[18] He is calling the entire culture into question, insisting that through this risen-from-the-dead Jesus, the whole world is being reorganized. And in this new reality, every person is equal. Everybody. Paul is the first person in the history of world literature to argue that all human beings are equal.[19]

Not only were these first Christians subverting the dominant power structures of their world, but they were confident that the resurrected Christ was working in them and through them to reclaim God's dream for the world. The writer Luke gives us insight into what this confidence looked like in their everyday lives. He wrote that they were witnessing the resurrection, "and God's grace was so powerfully at work in them all that there were no needy persons among them."[20] What was the result of the resurrection, according to Luke? "No needy persons among them."

Remember, the caesars claimed they were the ones who provided for everyone and saved everyone and made the world a better place. For these first Christians, the question was, Who is Lord? Jesus or Caesar? Who orders society? Who provides for you? Who puts food on your table? Who brings peace to the world?

To be a part of the church was to join a countercultural society that was partnering with God to create a new kind of culture, right under the nose of the caesars. These Christians made sure everybody in their midst had enough to eat. They made sure everybody was able to pay their bills. They made sure there was enough to go around. The resurrection for them was not an abstract spiritual concept; it was a concrete social and economic reality. God raised Jesus from the dead to show the world that Jesus is Lord, and it is through his power and his example and his Spirit that the world is restored.

It is important to remember that we rarely find these first Christians trying to prove that the resurrection actually occurred. For one, a lot of the people who saw Jesus after he rose from the dead were still alive, so if people had questions and doubts, they could talk to somebody who was actually there.[21] But there's another reason: Everybody's god in the first century had risen from the dead.[22] To claim a resurrection had occurred was nothing new: Julius Caesar himself was reported to have ascended to the right hand of the gods after his death. To try to prove there was an empty tomb wouldn't have gotten very far with the average citizen of the Roman Empire; they had heard it all before. This is why so many passages about the early church deal with possessions and meals and generosity.[23] They understood that people are rarely persuaded by arguments, but more often by experiences. Living, breathing, flesh-and-blood experiences of the resurrection community. They saw it as their responsibility to put Jesus's message on display. To the outside world, it was less about proving and more about inviting people to experience this community of Jesus's followers for themselves.

And so these first Christians passed on the faith to the next generation who passed it on to the next generation who passed it on to the next generation until it got to . . . us. Here. Today. Those who follow Jesus and belong to his church. And now it is our turn. It is our turn to step up and take responsibility for who the church is going to be for a new generation. It is our turn to redefine and reshape and dream it all up again. It is our turn to rediscover the beautiful, dangerous, compelling idea that a group of people, surrendered to God and to each other, really can change the world.

Serving Others

I am learning that the church is at its best when it gives itself away. And this is because blessing is always instrumental. Let me explain. In Genesis 12, God tells a man named Abram that he's going to bless him, and through him, he is going to bless the whole world. This is the birth of the Jewish people, whom God wants to use to reach everybody. This blessing is instrumental in nature. God wants to use Abraham, to flow through him, to have him be the conduit through whom God can bless everybody else.[24] Abraham is just a vessel. God doesn't choose people just so they'll feel good about themselves or secure in their standing with God or whatever else. God chooses people to be used to bless *other* people. Elected, predestined, chosen—whatever words people use for this reality, the point is never the person elected or chosen or predestined. The point is that person serving others, making their lives better.

The second significant idea in Genesis 12 is that Abraham's calling is universal. It is for everybody. All kinds of people all over the place are going to be blessed by God through Abraham. God has no boundaries. God blesses everybody. People who don't believe in God.

People who are opposed to God. People who do violent, evil things. God's intentions are to bless everybody. Jesus continues this idea in many of his teachings. In the book of Luke he says, "I am among you as one who serves."[25] He not only refers to himself as a servant, sent to serve others, but he teaches his disciples that the greatest in his kingdom are the ones who serve.[26] For Jesus, everything is upside down. The best and greatest and most important are the ones who humble themselves, set their needs and desires aside, and selflessly serve others.

So what is a group of people living this way called? That's the church. The church doesn't exist for itself; it exists to serve the world. It is not ultimately about the church; it's about all the people God wants to bless through the church. When the church loses sight of this, it loses its heart. This is especially true today in the world we live in where so many people are hostile to the church, many for good reason. We reclaim the church as a blessing machine not only because that is what Jesus intended from the beginning but also because serving people is the only way their perceptions of church are ever going to change. This is why it is so toxic for the gospel when Christians picket and boycott and complain about how bad the world is. This behavior doesn't help. It makes it worse. It isn't the kind of voice Jesus wants his followers to have in the world. Why blame the dark for being dark? It is far more helpful to ask why the light isn't as bright as it could be.

Good News

Another truth about the church we're embracing is that the gospel is good news, especially for those who don't believe it.

Imagine an average street in an average city in an average country, if there is such a place. Let's imagine Person X lives in a house on this street. Next door is a Hindu, and on the other side is a Muslim. Across the street is an atheist, next door to them an agnostic, and next door on the other side, someone from Ohio.

Imagine Person X becomes a Christian. Maybe she read something or had friends who inspired her to learn more, or maybe she had an addiction and through a recovery movement she surrendered her life to God. However it came to be, she became a follower of Jesus. Let's say she starts living out Jesus's teachings, actually taking him seriously that she can become a compelling force for good in the world. She is becoming more generous, more compassionate, more forgiving, more loving. Is she becoming a better or worse neighbor? If we are her neighbors, we're thrilled about her new faith. We find ourselves more and more grateful for a neighbor like this. We wish more people would be like this.

Let's make some observations about this street. The good news of Jesus is good news for Person X. It's good news for Person X's neighbors. It's good news for the whole street. It's good news for people who don't believe in Jesus. We have to be really clear about this. The good news for Person X is good news for the whole street. And if it is good news for the whole street, then it's good news for the whole world.

If the gospel isn't good news for everybody, then it isn't good news for anybody.

And this is because the most powerful things happen when the church surrenders its desire to convert people and convince them to join. It is when the church gives itself away in radical acts of service and compassion, expecting nothing in return, that the way of Jesus is most vividly put on display. To do this, the church must stop thinking about everybody primarily in categories of in or out, saved or not, believer or nonbeliever. Besides the fact that these terms are offensive to those who are the "un" and "non," they work against Jesus's teachings about how we are to treat each other. Jesus commanded us to love our neighbor, and our neighbor can be anybody.[27] We are all created in the image of God, and we are all sacred, valuable creations of God.[28] Everybody matters. To treat people differently based on who believes what is to fail to respect the image of God in everyone. As the book of James says, "God shows no favoritism."[29] So we don't either.

Oftentimes the Christian community has sent the message that we love people and build relationships in order to convert them to the Christian faith. So there is an agenda. And when there is an agenda, it isn't really love, is it? It's something else. We have to rediscover love, period. Love that loves because it is what Jesus teaches us to do. We have to surrender our agendas. Because some people aren't going to become Christians like us no matter how hard we push. They just aren't. And at some point we have to commit them to God, trusting that God loves them more than we ever could. I obviously love to talk to people about Jesus and my faith. I'll take every opportunity I can get. But I have learned that when I toss out my agenda and simply love as Jesus teaches me to, I often end up learning more about God than I could have imagined.

And one thing to keep in mind is that we never arrive. Ever. One of the illusions of faith is that at some point we get it all mapped out and things get smooth and predictable. It is not true. The way of Jesus is a journey, not a destination. On a journey, the scenery changes. A lot. We can prepare for some things but not all. We make mistakes, figure it out as we go along, and try new things. Failures are really just opportunities to learn. If you are part of a church, is the dominant understanding of faith in your church that of journey or destination?

I am learning that the church is at its best when it is underground, subversive, and countercultural. It is the quiet, humble, stealth acts that change things. I was just talking to a woman named Michelle who decided to move into the roughest neighborhood in our city to try to help people get out of the cycle of poverty and despair. She was telling me about the kids she is tutoring and the families they come from and how great the needs are. Some other women in our church heard about Michelle and asked her for lists of what exactly the families in her neighborhood need. (One of the families wrote on their list "heat.") They then circulated the lists until they found people who could meet every one of the needs. It's like an underground mom-mafia network. Michelle told me at last count they had helped 430 families, and they are making plans to expand their network.

"Jesus lives; here's a toaster."

These are the kinds of people who change the world. They improvise and adapt and innovate and explore new ways to get things done. They don't make a lot of noise, and they don't draw a lot of attention to themselves.

Difficulty, Suffering, and Hope

To be this kind of person—the kind who selflessly serves—takes everything a person has. It is difficult. It is demanding. And we often find ourselves going against the flow of those around us. Which is why we are reclaiming the simple fact that Jesus said the way is narrow.[30] We are honest about this, especially to our friends who wouldn't say they are Christians. Very few people in our world are offering anything worth dying for. Most of the messages we receive are about how to make life easier. The call of Jesus goes the other direction: It's about making our lives more difficult. It is going out of our way to be more generous and disciplined and loving and free. It is refusing to escape and become numb to and check out of this broken, fractured world.

And so we are embracing the high demands of Jesus's call to be one of his disciples. We are honest about it. We want our friends to know up front that the costs are high, which is what is so appealing about Jesus—his vision for life takes everything we have.

In the accounts of Jesus's life, often the larger the crowds get, the more demanding and difficult his teachings get. In John 6 he gives a teaching that is so hard to swallow, everybody but a few leave him. He is constantly trying to find out who really wants it. And so he keeps pushing and prodding and questioning and putting it out there until some leave and the diehards stay. We never find him chasing after someone, trying to convince them that he really wasn't that serious, that it was just a figure of speech. He didn't really mean sell your possessions and give to the poor. If anybody didn't have a Messiah complex, it was Jesus.

This is what we are all dying for—something that demands we step up and become better, more focused people. Something that calls out the greatness that we hope is somewhere inside of us.

Not only is the way narrow, but it involves suffering. To truly engage with how the world is, our hearts are going to be broken again and again. Just this past week, I met a woman who is terrified her husband is going to beat her, and another woman who has a degenerative muscle disease that is causing her face to freeze up, and I can think of at least five couples who are splitting up, and . . . you get the picture. It is your world too. And so we are learning how to suffer well. Not to avoid it but to feel the full force of it. It is important that churches acknowledge suffering and engage it—never, ever presenting the picture that if you follow Jesus, your problems will go away. Following Jesus may bring on problems you never imagined.

Suffering is a place where clichés don't work and words often fail. I was at lunch last week with a friend who is in the middle of some difficult days, and I don't have any answers. I just don't. I can't fix it for him. I've tried. And we sat there and talked and ate, and I let him know that I'm in it with him. It isn't very pretty and it isn't very fun, but when we join each other in the pain and confusion, God is there. Sometimes it means we sit in silence for a while, not knowing what to say. And it is in our suffering together that we find out we are not alone. We find out who really loves us. We find out that with these people around us, we can make it through anything. And that gives us something to celebrate.

Ultimately our gift to the world around us is hope. Not blind hope that pretends everything is fine and refuses to acknowledge how things are. But the kind of hope that comes from staring pain and suffering right in the eyes and refusing to believe that this is all there is. It is what we all need—hope that comes not from going around suffering but from going through it. I am learning that the church has nothing to say to the world until it throws better parties. By this I don't necessarily mean balloons and confetti and clowns who paint faces. I mean back-yards and basements and porches. It is in the flow of real life, in the places we live and move with the people we're on the journey with, that we are reminded it is God's world and we're going to be okay.

Central to reclaiming creation and being a resurrection community is the affirmation that when God made the world, God said it was "good."

And it still is.

Food and music and art and friends and stories and rivers and lakes and oceans and laughter and . . . did I mention food? God has given us life, and God's desire is that we live it. It is the job of the church to lead the world in affirming and, more important, enjoying the goodness of creation. We are not going somewhere else at the end of time, because this world is our home. And our home is good.

One of the most tragic things ever to happen to the gospel was the emergence of the message that Jesus takes us somewhere else if we believe in him. The Bible ends with God coming here.[31] God, in the midst of all the people who can imagine nothing better, celebrating the life that we all share. The images Jesus used were of banquets and feasts and celebrations.[32] What do we do at parties such as these? We eat and talk and dance and enjoy each other and above all else, we take our time. What does Jesus do almost as much as he teaches and heals? He eats long meals. As Christians, it is our duty to master the art of the long meal.

If you find yourself wanting to take me less seriously, let me ask a question: What was the ritual the first Christians observed with the most frequency? Exactly. The common meal, also called the Eucharist or the Lord's Supper. And what did this meal consist of? Hours of talking and sharing and enjoying each other's presence. Food is the basis of life, it comes from the earth, and the earth is God's. In a Jewish home in Jesus's day—and even now—the table is seen as an altar. It's holy. Time spent around the table with each other is time spent with God.

My wife and I threw a party last summer and we called it "An Epic Celebration of All That Is Good." We had a band playing in the backyard and food everywhere, a DJ set up in the living room, all the furniture was pushed against the walls, and there were cars up and down the street—and it was just the best. And what was the occasion for the party? I was hoping you'd ask. There wasn't one. That's the best reason you can have. Relax. Slow down. Quit having a purpose for everything. Eat more slowly and enjoy it more. Ask people how they are doing—and mean it. Take more walks. You will get more done anyway.

She

One of the central metaphors for God and his people throughout the Bible is that of a groom and his bride. God is the groom; his people are the bride. I like this because it makes the church a "she." We need to reclaim this image.

The church is a she.

She's a mystery, isn't she? Still going after all this time. After the Crusades and the Inquisition and Christian cable television. Still going. And there continue to be people like me who believe she is one of the best ideas ever. In spite of all the ways she has veered off track. In spite of all the people who have actually turned away from God because of what they experienced in church. I am starting to realize why: The church is like a double-edged sword. When it's good, when it's on, when it's right, it's like nothing on earth. A group of people committed to selflessly serving and loving the world around them? Great. But when it's bad, all that potential gets turned the other way. From the highest of highs to the lowest of lows. Sometimes in the same week. Sometimes in the same day.

But she will live on. She's indestructible. When she dies in one part of the world, she explodes in another. She's global. She's universal. She's everywhere. And while she's fragile, she's going to endure. In every generation there will be those who see her beauty and give their lives to see her shine. Jesus said the gates of hell will not prevail against her. That's strong language. And it's true. She will continue to roll across the ages, serving and giving and connecting people with God and each other. And people will abuse her and manipulate her and try to control her, but they'll pass on. And she will keep going.

EPILOGUE

One summer when I was in high school, my family and I were on vacation and decided to visit a church in the town where we were staying. At the end of the service, the pastor asked if anybody wanted to become a Christian. He said that people could repeat a prayer after him and become a Christian, right there at that moment in their seats. He said that if people repeated this prayer after him, they could be sure that when they died, they would go to heaven and not hell. He then asked everybody to bow their heads and close their eyes, and he said the prayer, leaving space after each sentence for those who wanted to repeat the prayer after him. When he finished, he told everybody to keep their eyes closed and heads bowed. He then asked for the people who had prayed the prayer to raise their hands wherever they were seated. This way he would know who they were so he could pray for them. He said that nobody but him would be looking.

The pastor then said, "I see that hand over there. Thank you. I see a hand in the back. I see some young women in the front . . ." And he proceeded to acknowledge the hands that were going up all around the room.

During this entire time I had kept my eyes open and was watching the whole thing.

I didn't see any hands go up.

Several years ago my dad reminded me of that day. He told me he had his eyes open the whole time as well— only he was not watching for hands. He was watching me. He said that when he realized what was going on and that I was observing it all, he had this sick feeling that I would walk away from God and the church and faith forever. He said he kept thinking, *I've lost Rob. I've lost Rob . . .*

I am like you. I have seen plenty done in the name of God that I'm sure God doesn't want anything to do with. I have lots of reasons for bailing on the whole thing.

I am also like you because I have a choice. To become bitter, cynical, jaded, and hard. Anybody can do that. A lot have. Hatred is a powerful, unifying force. And there is a lot to be repulsed by.

Or, like you, I can choose to reclaim my innocence. We can choose to reclaim our innocence together. We can insist that hope is real and that a group of people who love God and others really can change the world. We can reclaim our idealism and our belief and our confidence in the big ideas that stir us deep in our bones. We can commit all the more to being the kinds of people who are learning how to do what Jesus teaches us.

I am not going to stop dreaming of a new kind of faith for the millions of us who need it. I am not going to stop dreaming of new kinds of communities that put the love of God and the brilliance of Jesus on display in honest, compelling ways. I am not going to stop dreaming of new ways to live lives of faith and creativity and meaning and significance.

But I can't do it alone. I need you. We need you. We need you to rediscover wonder and awe. We need you to believe that it is really possible. We need you to join us.

It's better that way.
It's what Jesus had in mind.

ENDNOTES

MOVEMENT ONE **JUMP**

1 Marcus Borg explains this idea extremely well in his book *The Heart of Christianity* (San Francisco: HarperSanFrancisco, 2003).

2 John 14:9.

3 I first came across the phrase "lined up" in Cornelius Plantinga's book *Engaging God's World* (Grand Rapids: Eerdmans, 2002).

4 John 1:14.

5 This fact, of course, doesn't make the doctrine any less true. It's been true all along; people just "recently" discovered it.

6 Deuteronomy 4:12; see also verse 15.

7 Job 11:7. God also says in Isaiah 55:8, "My thoughts are not your thoughts, neither are your ways my ways." It is written like this in the Psalms: "His understanding has no limit" (147:5).

8 Exodus 3:14.

9 Exodus 33:23.

10 It's interesting that we measure days by the sun and moon, which weren't created until day four.

11 Matthew 19:28; Acts 3:21; Colossians 1:20.

12 See Matthew 25:41.

13 Luke 14:16–24.

14 David Rylaarsdam from Calvin Theological Seminary makes a
    great point about questioning God: In Job 42:7, God indicates
    that he is angry with the questions of Job's three friends, which
    is paralleled in the gospels when the religious leaders try to trap
    Jesus with their questions. But Job's friends and the Pharisees
    had a smug sense of arrival about their theology. The psalmists,
    by contrast, demonstrate *humility* about their understanding of
    God, and their questions arise out of the context of *faith* (even if it
    is weak faith mixed with much doubt). So the psalmists are able to
    ask even tougher questions of God than the Pharisees: "My God,
    my God, you said you would not forget your children, and now
    you're hiding your face from me. I don't get it! Where are you? I'm
    getting hammered here. Why?"

15 Genesis 18.

16 Exodus 3–4.

17 Take a look at *I Asked for Wonder: A Spiritual Anthology* by
    Abraham Joshua Heschel, edited by Samuel Dresner (New York:
    Crossroad Classic, 1983).

18 Robert Farrar Capon deals with this in his book *The Fingerprints
    of God* (Grand Rapids: Eerdmans, 2000). Go out and buy all of his
    books and read them immediately.

19 If you really want to know, this is from M. Night Shyamalan's *The
    Sixth Sense* (1999).

20 1 John 4:8, my emphasis.

21 This is quoted from *Entertainment Weekly* (6 February 2004).

22 I heard Dwight Pryor say this several years ago. Dwight is about
    as close as you can get to a Christian rabbi, and he has deeply
    influenced me. Check out his teachings at www.jcstudies.com.

23 David Rylaarsdam provided me with this insight.

24 Read everything John Piper has ever written, beginning with *The Dangerous Duty of Delight* (Sisters, OR: Multnomah, 2001).

25 Psalm 37:4.

26 Matthew 7:13–14.

27 Philippians 4:7.

MOVEMENT TWO **YOKE**

1 Joshua 6.

2 2 Corinthians 11:23.

3 1 Corinthians 7:12.

4 1 Corinthians 7:4.

5 Leviticus 19:18.

6 Exodus 20:8.

7 Matthew 11:30.

8 Matthew 5:17.

9 My version of Jesus's words in Matthew 5.

10 Matthew 3:11.

11 Matthew 3:17.

12 Matthew 3.

13 Luke 20:2–3, my paraphrase.

14 Matthew 5:21–22, 27–28, 31–32, 33–34, 38–39, 43–44.

15 See *Anchor Bible Dictionary* 1.743–45 (New York: Doubleday, 1992) and Walter Bauer et al. *A Greek-English Lexicon of the New*

Testament and Other Early Christian Literature, 3rd ed. (Chicago: University of Chicago Press, 2000), 222.

Also, according to Josephus, "The power of binding and loosing was always claimed by the Pharisees. Under Queen Alexandra, the Pharisees became the administrators of all public affairs so as to be empowered to banish and readmit whom they pleased, as well as to loose and to bind" (*Wars of the Jews*, 1.5.2 in *The Complete Works of Josephus,* trans. by William Whiston [Grand Rapids: Kregel, 1960]).

To read more about binding and loosing, go to the Jerusalem Perspective website: www.jerusalemperspective.com.

16 Matthew 16:19; see also 18:18.

17 Acts 15:28–29.

18 Matthew 18:20.

19 I heard Anne Lamott say this at an event we were both speaking at.

20 Romans 16:16; 1 Corinthians 16:20; 2 Corinthians 13:12; 1 Thessalonians 5:26.

21 1 Corinthians 11:3–16.

22 1 Corinthians 16:22.

23 Matthew 19:21.

24 1 Timothy 2:8.

25 Ephesians 6:5.

26 Acts 15:28.

27 Genesis 3.

28 "There are seventy faces/facets to the Torah" (*Numbers Rabbah* 13:15).

29 John 11:39.

30 Once again, Marcus Borg does a great job of explaining this idea in *The Heart of Christianity* (San Francisco: HarperSanFrancisco, 2003).

31 The best thing I have ever read about the Bible is a transcript of a lecture given by the British scholar N. T. Wright called "How Can the Bible Be Authoritative?" published in *Vox Evangelica* 21 (April 1991): 7–32.

32 The tractate in the Mishnah, "Avot," is very helpful in understanding what the debates were and what was forbidden and what was permitted in Jesus's day.

33 And the answer is . . . Shammai. Which is interesting, because Jesus usually sides with Hillel.

34 For more on Artemis and her role in the city of Ephesus, check out Roland H. Worth Jr.'s *The Seven Cities of the Apocalypse and Greco-Asian Culture* (New York: Paulist Press, 1999).

35 Again, read the transcript by N. T. Wright, "How Can the Bible Be Authoritative?"

36 2 Peter 3:16.

37 I understand the need to ground all that we do and say in the Bible, which is my life's work. It is the belief that creeps in sometimes that this book dropped out of the sky that is dangerous. The Bible has come to us out of actual communities of people, journeying in real time and space. Guided by a real Spirit.

38 As Stanley Gundry put it so well: The formation of the canon was a long, dynamic, and fluid process and one that was not ever settled once and for all by any one body of individuals voting on it and settling it for future generations of Christians (except that for Roman Catholics it was officially settled at the Council of Trent in the sixteenth century, though even many Roman Catholics challenge its decisions!). Protestants accept the narrower Hebrew canon accepted by the Jews at the time of Christ (the Law, the Prophets, and the Writings). Books aspiring to be accepted as the uniquely Christian scriptures are to be subjected to the tests of authenticity and apostolicity. By contrast, the Roman Catholic tradition is that since the church wrote the Bible, the church also has the authority to determine which books belong in the Bible, and only the church can give an authoritative interpretation of the Bible.

The Protestant position has been that in general the people of God have come to accept certain books as God's Word because through the centuries God's children have heard the voice of their Father speaking in these books. So when we point to early lists of the canonical books, whether such lists come from individuals or church councils, these lists are not considered authoritative decisions binding on us today but only as evidence that a loose consensus was developing through time among the people of God.

Given this reality, it is not surprising that while there is general agreement on what belongs in the canon, there is no uniform agreement.

Remember, it's living and active.

MOVEMENT THREE **TRUE**

1 Isaiah 6:3.

2 Psalm 24:1.

3 Psalm 139:7.

4 Genesis 28:16.

5 Romans 2:14.

6 Titus 1:12–13.

7 Acts 17:28.

8 1 Corinthians 3:21, 23.

9 Colossians 1:17.

10 John 14:6.

11 Colossians 2:17.

12 Colossians 3:17.

13 1 Timothy 4:4.

14 Psalm 24:1.

15 1 Peter 5:8.

16 1 Thessalonians 5:21.

17 Acts 14:17.

18 Matthew 26:10 and Mark 14:6.

19 At that point I was thinking that she could start a recovery group for witches. It could be called "WA" for Witches Anonymous.

20 Exodus 3:5.

MOVEMENT FOUR **TASSELS**

1 Numbers 15:38–40.

2 David cuts off the corner of Saul's "garment" in the back of a cave (1 Sam. 24:4), and Jesus talks about going into your "prayer closet," which meant folding your prayer shawl over your head and arms (Matt. 6:6).

3 Malachi 4:2 NIV (Colorado Springs: International Bible Society, 1978, 1984).

4 Luke 8:43–48.

5 The first time I heard Dwight Pryor address this, he made two columns and explained the difference between a legal transaction understanding and a holistic understanding and said that we need to embrace both. I thought I was going to fall out of my chair. He is the one who uses the phrase "the cross for us and the cross in us." He sponsors seminars he calls "Haverim" (from the Hebrew word for "friends") at which he teaches for a week. Every day, all day he

teaches, and it is stunning. Check his website www.jcstudies.com for where he will be teaching next.

6 John 5:24.

7 Ephesians 1:10.

8 For a masterful depiction of the mystery behind the mystery, read Susan Howatch. I recommend starting with *Glittering Images* (New York: Knopf, 1987), the first of her Starbridge novels. You will get sucked in and have to read her next eight novels.

9 Parker Palmer's book *Let Your Life Speak* (San Francisco: Jossey-Bass, 1999) was my introduction to this great man.

10 Mark 8:36.

MOVEMENT FIVE **DUST**

1 *Bava Batra* 21a.

2 Josephus, *Against Apion* 1:60.

3 The person who has opened me up to the first century world of Jesus more than anyone is Ray Vander Laan. He is a teacher, scholar, hiker of Israel—an amazing man. His teachings are available at www.followtherabbi.com, an exhaustive resource for those interested in Jesus's world. The levels of education and the walking on water and the Caesarea sections in this movement were insights sparked by things I've heard Ray say. Much credit goes to the man from Hamilton.

4 Luke 2:46-47.

5 See John 15:15.

6 For a fascinating glimpse into what this looked like, read *As a Driven Leaf* by Milton Steinberg (New York: Behrman, 1996), a novel about rabbis and disciples.

7 Matthew 4:18-22.

8 Google "Caesarea Philippi" and you will see what I mean.

9 John 15:16.

10 Matthew 17:14–20.

11 Matthew 28:19.

MOVEMENT SIX **NEW**

1 Luke 11:46.

2 Matthew 23:13.

3 James 3:2.

4 Romans 3:23.

5 John 3:3.

6 Colossians 3:3.

7 Colossians 3:1.

8 Colossians 3:7; see also Ephesians 4:20–24.

9 2 Corinthians 5:17.

10 Hebrews 2:10; 5:9.

11 Colossians 3:12.

12 Philippians 3:16.

13 Romans 8:1.

14 John 17:21.

15 Romans 6:11.

16 John 5:24.

17 You must read *The Divine Conspiracy* by Dallas Willard (San Francisco: HarperSanFrancisco, 1998).

18 I heard Stuart Briscoe say this to a group of people in Milwuakee in 1997.

19 "Sin management" is a term Dallas Willard deals with extensively in the second chapter of his book *The Divine Conspiracy,* which everybody should have read by now.

20 Luke 15:11–31.

21 Romans 5:8.

22 Revelation 5:9.

23 John 12:32.

24 See Colossians 1:20.

25 Matthew 25:31–46.

26 Genesis 3:8–9.

27 Exodus 25.

28 John 1:14 in *The Message* (Colorado Springs: NavPress, 1993).

29 1 Corinthians 6:19; Ephesians 2:21–22.

30 Revelation 21–22.

31 Matthew 4:17.

32 Romans 8:37–39.

MOVEMENT SEVEN **GOOD**

1 John 20:15.

2 Take, for example, the genealogy that begins the book of Matthew. It appears to be a list of people who did a lot of begetting. But there's something else going on here. The greatest king of the Jews was David. In Hebrew, that's spelled DVD. *D* is the fourth letter in the Hebrew alphabet, so it has the numerical value of 4. *V* is the sixth letter, so it has the value of 6. DVD is therefore 4 + 6

+ 4, which gives the name David the number value of 14. Matthew groups the names in his genealogy in groups of . . . 14. So a Jew reading the introduction to his book, which is telling something about Jesus's family, would read king, king, king, king, king. Matthew has an agenda here. He wants you to see who he thinks Jesus is.

3 Romans 5:12.

4 Acts 2:24.

5 For a mind-blowing introduction to emergence theory and divine creativity, set aside three months and read Ken Wilber's *A Brief History of Everything* (Boston: Shambhala, 2001).

6 A writer who has helped me in understanding this difference between good and perfect, and more important, between Greek and Hebrew thought, is Thorleif Boman. His book *Hebrew Thought Compared with Greek* (New York: Norton, 2002) has been very helpful. Brian McLaren also writes about this in *The Story We Find Ourselves In* (San Francisco: Jossey-Bass, 2003). I love his explanation of the Genesis account of creation. Or should I say Neo's?

7 See Cornelius Plantinga's book *Engaging God's World* (Grand Rapids: Eerdmans, 2002).

8 Romans 8:22.

9 Isaiah 66.

10 Matthew 19:28.

11 Acts 3:21.

12 Colossians 1:19–20.

13 1 Corinthians 15:20.

14 *Christ and the Caesars* by Ethelbert Stauffer (London: SCM, 1952) is the best book I have come across on Jesus and the Roman Empire. Stunning piece of work. I'd also recommend Richard Horsley's *Jesus and Empire* (Minneapolis: Fortress, 2003).

15 Acts 4.

16 It's interesting that the word *church* was originally used by Christians as an intentionally political statement about who rules the world.

17 Acts 4:12.

18 Galatians 3:28.

19 Thomas Cahill talks about this fact in *The Desire of the Everlasting Hills* (New York: Anchor, 2001). This is one of the best books I've read about the early church.

20 Acts 4:34.

21 1 Corinthians 15.

22 For an example of this, find a book on Greek mythology and look up Dionysus, also called Bacchus.

23 The entire book of Acts.

24 At first he is called Abram, but then God changes his name to Abraham. See Genesis 17:5.

25 Luke 22:27.

26 John 13 is a powerful example of this.

27 Jesus is actually giving commentary on Torah in his loving your neighbor command, specifically Leviticus 19.

28 Genesis 1:26–27.

29 See James 2:1–13.

30 Matthew 7:14.

31 Revelation 21–22.

32 Luke 15; John 2 and 14.